FROM BONDAGE TO LIBERTY

Abused But Still Anointed

FROM BONDAGE TO LIBERTY

Abused But Still Anointed

Lakeia M. Smith

Copyright © 2020 by Lakeia M. Smith

All rights reserved

Publisher's Note
No part of this book may be reproduced, stored in or introduced into a retrieval system, or transmitted, in any form or by any means (electronic, mechanical, photocopying, recording, or otherwise) without prior written permission from the playwright and/or heirs.

ISBN: 9781658068758

Scriptures used in this publication are quoted from the *Amplified® Bible* (AMP), Copyright ©2015 by The Lockman Foundation. Used by permission; the King James Version - Bible in Public Domain; and the New International Version (NIV) Holy Bible, New International Version®, NIV® Copyright ©1973, 1978, 1984, 2011 by Biblica, Inc.® Used by permission.

Published by Lakeia M. Smith

For information on this publication, please contact lakeia0@gmail.com

WrightStuf Consulting, LLC
www.wrightstuf.com

Printed in the United States of America

Dedication

I dedicate this book, to several strong women who helped me endure some of the darkest days of my life; my mother, Reshelle Gainor, my godmother Tonya Green, my spiritual mother Gigi Turner, my Grandmother Linda Jackson, and the world greatest Auntie Larchardon Moore A.K.A Aunt Punkin. I love you all dearly. Thank you for all the encouragement, prayers, and many sacrifices you've given from my childhood days until today. I would not be the woman of God I am without you.

Thank you for loving me in spite of my mistakes. Thank you for encouraging me and praying for me when I wanted to give up, and thank you for never judging me but always seeing and knowing that God had a plan for my life, and he would use me one day to help others. Each of you have been through very dark storms of your own, and I'm blessed to have witnessed the strength you carry. Watching how you've handled your storms, encouraged me to have strength through mine. I love you all very much.

Thank You,
Your Daughter, Grand-Daughter, & Niece,

Lakeia Smith

Encouragement Words from Godmother

"In Need of Love"

My story is simple and true-minded. After having much difficulty becoming pregnant, this blessing came into my life by way of a different means. My mother, Mae B. Green, became the proud grandmother. She loved this baby and I loved her as my own. I took pride in being a God-Mother to a baby who already had siblings, a mother and father. I didn't care. I knew I was there to help. Lakeia became a big part of my heart and my life. I loved dressing her up. She was loved by her church family. She was the healing blessing I needed to move on.

I have a lot of God-Children and I am a part of their lives. Special is a word for them all. Being young, I didn't know what to do but put my faith in action. Lakeia sang in the choir, she was an usher, and she loved the way I dressed her. Her hair was always in place, chap-stick for the lips; I was raising a little, a woman who would be fearfully and wonderfully made. I made sure her stockings and socks were put on right. Grandma Mae Bell wouldn't have it any other way.

Lakeia loved shoes with a little heel. Nothing but the best for all my little ones. I taught them all to be a family. Her smile was infectious, and she wore it well. Her eyes twinkled when she looked at me. She made my heart very happy. I loved my Lakeia with all my heart. Daily blessings were a part of our getting ready for the day. One day, I dropped her off at school and I was rushing out of her class to leave for work, and Lakeia began to cry "MOMMY", I said what? "I can't leave without my blessing." I stopped, prayed, and anointed her head with oil, she immediately calmed down and was able to proceed in school. I thought about this later, and knew I had to protect this child with the help of the Lord.

One Sunday morning, I remember looking down at Lakeia and tears rolled down her face. She would sing and cry to "This is my story, this is my song, praising my savior all the daylong". I knew then she was a special child. No one knew she would become a woman who is fearfully and wonderfully made. Now this is her story and no matter what the enemy tried to do to block her blessings he could not win. God says in Jeremiah 29:11, "For I know the plans I have for you," declares the LORD, "plans to prosper you and not to harm you, plans to give you hope and a future…

God knew his plans for her life. You can't run from God. He knows the beginning and the end. In this life, we will fall but be of good cheer. God has made a way.

Love you Lakeia. My life is of the better because you were in my life. Congratulations on this blessed book! I am proud to be your God-Mother!

Mama Tonya

Table of Contents

Foreword	i
Introduction	iii
Chapter 1 ~ Lost	1
Chapter 2 ~ Painful Transition	13
Chapter 3 ~ Broken	21
Chapter 4 ~ Fighting for Life	37
Chapter 5 ~ Confused	45
Chapter 6 ~ The Pressing of Faith Activated	55
Chapter 7 ~ It's Time to Fight Back	67
Chapter 8 ~ Me Vs. ME	83
Chapter 9 ~ Healed –	103
Twenty Nuggets of Wisdom	105

Foreword

During the time my daughter, Lakeia, was writing this book, I had some concerns that she was not aware of. Concerns about what she was going to say about me in the book. The enemy had begun to filtrate my mind with shame for not fulfilling the ideology of what I think a mother should have been to a daughter. These feelings were trying to take over before I read the book.

On a Monday morning in December 2019, I received the text of the name of the book, which brought excitement and curiosity, and immediately, as I read the title, I felt freedom from those concerns and peace. It was as if the title alone was for me. I even responded to her with a "Thank you." If the title alone brought me freedom, I was sure the book would be a powerful tool for deliverance.

After reading her story, it challenged me to reflect upon areas of my life to understand the patterns that take place with choices we make and the influence it has on our children and others. As a mother, knowing what I know now, if I had to do it all over again, things would be done differently. That's the love I have for my daughter. Reading what she endured, cause mixed emotions, which is natural for me to feel, after all, she is my daughter and friend.

Therefore, her story took me to place with God in soul-searching and prayer that gave me a better understanding of how to get free (forgive), stay free (love), and have better relationships. This book showed me that God loves us and even when it looks like all hell is breaking loose on us, God's word is true that "All things works for the good of those who love him..." (Romans 8:28). This book is sure evidence that there is a purpose for the storms and pain.

Regardless of where you are in your own personal, spiritual, or emotional journey, I am convinced you will be both encouraged, challenged, and set free by this book. Its message is clear and powerful to lead you to Christ Jesus and the deliverance you need when you pray the prayers and write your reflections of you own situations.

From Bondage to Liberty... Abused but still Anointed is the most powerful book I have ever read. It re-ignited a passion within me to search my own heart for any hidden pain or hurt, and seek God for pure forgiveness and love. I encourage you to take time during the reflections and be honest with yourself to obtain your healing and deliverance. This book assured me that GOD IS REAL!

My hope is that you take quality time and read this book. You will open up not only your mind but your heart to the life-changing ways of dealing with difficult situations and principles of God within that will change your pattern of thinking about yourself and others.

Prophetess Reshelle Gainor
Wife, Mother, Preacher, Teacher of Special Education

Introduction

If someone were to ask me, "Has your life been a struggle, as a young lady with dreams, and are you where you expected to be right now versus when you were younger and in school?" I would honestly reply, "Not at all". When we are young, we have huge dreams of being princesses, being rich, having huge houses, becoming doctors, lawyers, police officers, and even the president of the United States. The world looks so big from a child's eyes and it looks as if anything is possible; and anything is possible if you believe. Yet there is an opposite side, such as life's unknown obstacles, heart breaks, disappointments, and learning everyone is not for you, or loves you.

When I was a young girl, no one told me that as beautiful as the world seemed, there was an ugly side too. It was not until I grew up and stepped out into this world that I saw how ugly it could be. But the wonderful thing about running into ugly, hurtful pain, I found beauty in the brokenness, and as you continue to read this book, you will also find that in all you've been through and all you're going through, there is beauty that's birth out of your pain.

So, in the future when adversity comes, you will see the beauty in the pain. The best part is you will no longer consider it as pain, and those things which seemed to hurt you will no longer have a painful effect on you.

I pray when you are done with this book, the weight on your shoulders will be gone, you will walk in true forgiveness. You will love yourself more than ever. You will love those that hurt you, but most of all, you will have an everlasting deep un-removable, unshakable love for Christ Jesus.

Chapter 1 ~ Lost

When my family moved to Augusta, Georgia in 2005, I thought it was the worst mistake ever. My mom married a pastor who relocated us from North Carolina to an unfamiliar place in Georgia. He moved my youngest brother, my mom and me. He encouraged my mother to quit her job and told her he would take care of us, and of course that being her husband, she believed him. He leased a 2-story house with 4 bedrooms, 2 ½ baths, a beautiful front yard and an amazing backyard that was right by a pond where we could fish. It was definitely a beautiful home, and we moved during the summer, so the weather was perfect. I loved the scenery and the home, yet I was not at peace. I was unhappy inside, I didn't want to leave my home, I didn't want to leave my family and friends. I'd just graduated from high school, and I wanted time to enjoy myself living in my hometown.

After we had completed moving into the new home, my mother's husband left. He did not leave us with food or money, and neither my mom nor I had a job. So here my stepfather, whose occupation was a truck driver, moves my entire family to another state, only to abandon us. This situation made me angrier and bitter. I was angry with my mom because I never wanted to leave NC and I was even angrier at this man who was preaching the love of Christ but acted differently. I could not understand why he abandoned us. So, we were forced to move out of the house. My mom eventually was offered a truck driving job because she had a Commercial Driver's License (CDL) also. Although it was an awesome blessing that she finally found work, the job required her to travel and be away from home a lot. With us not having family in Augusta, my youngest brother and I had to move into a stranger's house. The owner was a sweet Caucasian woman whom my mother met through a friend. My mother had to work and the quickest way for her to make money, save money, and provide for my baby brother and I was by traveling on the road driving trucks.

So, for about a year, we were with this lady who we didn't know, while my mom continued to send money home to provide for us. I hated my situation and I was angry at my mother for putting me in it. I rebelled against her and everything else. I did things I'd never done before, and things my mother would have never allowed me to do. I hung out late, dated guys I knew my mother wouldn't approve of. I still went to church because my mom would call just to see if my brother and I had attended church. And to me that's exactly what we did, attended church to be checked off the attendance list. We attended a mega church at the time. It was easy to live a sinful life and go to that church because no one ever noticed me. I felt invisible. The message that was preached never moved my brother or me. We checked in and checked out so when my mom called, we could honestly say we attended church.

During my rebellious period I started dating this guy. For the sake of privacy, we will call him EJ. EJ was handsome; seemed strong, and dangerous. We met at a restaurant where we both worked. We started hanging out late and eventually those long late nights turned into nights of sin. We fell into our lustful desires and I conceived my first son. In all honesty, I was in a state of denial for a time, even though every test I took came back positive. My mother sensed I was pregnant and kept telling me I was. After five positive pregnancy tests, including the one from my obstetrician (OB-GYN), I finally accepted that I was pregnant. I told EJ first, and he wanted me to have an abortion. I couldn't do that, and I let him know; under no uncertain terms, absolutely not. By this time, my mother had found a home for us to live in. It was a four-bedroom, 2 ½ bath home. She was still driving trucks to provide for us, so she was hardly at home.

My mother and I eventually had the conversation about me marrying the father of my child because she was not about to allow us to be together in her home unmarried. His mother had voiced a similar sentiment about us living in her home because she did not want to set a bad example for her daughter. I wasn't ready for marriage and neither was he, but I chose to marry because I couldn't see myself not being with the father of my child. I beat myself up about it for a while, I didn't want to be a single mom. I desired family, the father expressed how much he loved me and said he wanted his family together, so we married one month before the baby was due to be born.

This was the beginning of a life I never thought I would experience. Less than a month after our wedding day, he had cheated. During the birthing of my child, EJ was entertaining a relationship with another woman. This is when I first learned how to really bury pain and try to ignore what I really felt on the inside. While preparing to push, EJ would converse with the other woman on the phone and tell her everything that was going on with me. I asked him if he would get off the phone with her, he replied get out my face and walked out of my hospital room. I couldn't believe what was happening to me. Tears rolled down my face while I laid there numb in my spirit and numb physically. My mother and his mother walked in and saw me crying. My mom asked what was wrong and I replied, "Nothing."

They thought I was crying because I was scared of giving birth, but I was crying because I was heartbroken. In my mind I told myself, this is not how it's supposed to be when you bring another life into the world. I thought this man loved me. Although my mother did not know what was going on with me internally, she knew I was upset. She read the bible to me to help comfort me.

This is where the internal battle really began for me. EJ cheated on me numerous times after that, but yet I stayed. I contended with low self-esteem and had major insecurities about myself. I thought that maybe he cheated so much because I didn't have the biggest butt or breast. I felt this way because I would constantly hear him talk about how thick other women were. I told myself he didn't want me because my body wasn't fit to be loved or embraced by a man. "You don't have the Coca Cola shape he desires." I told myself God made a mistake when he created me. *I'm a skinny girl weighing 114 lbs. and I don't look like the girls on the video's or on the porn tapes that EJ liked to watch.* I disliked myself more and more and I despised what I saw in the mirror when I stood in front of it. These feelings caused me to not look at myself in the mirror much because I did not like who was looking back at me. I didn't' think I deserved better, so I worked and took care of my family. I was the provider. While I was providing, he would go out to the club, get drunk, and would call me from the club while I was in the bed sleeping with my son and accuse me of cheating. I was not allowed to have friends. If I had a guy friend, I was accused of sleeping with him, and if I had a female friend, I was accused of being a homosexual, or she had me sleeping with other guys. Therefore, to prevent arguments, I never went anywhere, didn't have friends, and always lived in fear of what could happen to me if I tried.

At that time, I did not feel I had a close relationship with God, but I always knew that no matter what I could pray. I'd seen my grandmother, godmother, and my biological mother pray, so no matter what I would go through, I still prayed. I asked God every day to help me stay in my right mind. I needed to stay strong for my son and for me. Although I would get cursed at, called different names, and cheated on continuously, I still wouldn't leave. I would ask myself "What is wrong with you? Why are you staying in this? What is holding you here?" I was bound by shame and guilt; I was oppressed and depressed. So, I chose to suffer because I felt I deserved this because I got pregnant out of wedlock. I felt like I was a disappointment to my mom, as well.

The verbal and mental abuse continued until it became physical. One night, EJ and I went out to bowl with his friends. He became very drunk. EJ was already a very jealous man and, drinking alcohol intensified his jealous emotions. His friends and I noticed his behavior getting out of hand. We recognized it was time to go. I feared him because of the things he would do while drunk, and the things he would say to me while sober. Right before leaving the bowling alley, EJ saw his friend and me talking. His friend asked me how his fiancé could get a job where I worked because she was seeking employment. I provided him the information, a totally innocent conversation. EJ became furious, jacked me up on the wall, walked me outside, and choked me until I had fingerprints around my neck. He grabbed me in the headlock and drove off with my face stuck in between his legs. During the ride, he beat my face against the window and the dashboard until I was numb, he bit me, and continue to choke me. He beat my head and face against the radio until I had the knob imprints pressed into my face. He stuffed my face between his legs, and I rode in this position all the way to his mother's house. I'd fought back until I couldn't move. I thought I was going to die that night. I remember praying to the Lord while he was choking me and trying to suffocate me. I told the Lord, "If I die, don't let me die like this."

Isaiah 41:10-13 *Fear thou not; for I am with thee: be not dismayed; for I am thy God: I will strengthen thee; yea I will help thee; yea I will uphold thee with the right hand of my righteousness (KJV).*

I asked him to help me and let me live. I begin to feel myself blacking out. I was weak and as my eyes faded and my breathing slowed down, the car stopped. EJ's door opened and I found enough strength to crawl out of his lap onto the ground gasping for air. I screamed for help, and his mother came out running. I got off the ground and ran to her screaming "He's trying to kill me" He attacked me again inside her house; he choked me, picked me up as high as he could, and slammed me on the ground as hard as he could. The body slam knocked the wind out of me. I felt as if my life left my body. I laid there hurt, broken, confused, and in pain. I could not understand why I was allowing myself to go through such abuse. He eventually went to jail for what he had done, but as soon as he got out I accepted him back.

What is wrong with me? I would ask myself over and over; God why am I going through this foolishness? Why can't I have better, why do I feel ashamed, lonely, guilty, and dark on the inside? I always knew how to pray but I still felt so far from God. However, no matter what I was going through, I still forced myself to go to church. One day my mother took me to visit City of Life Ministries in Grovetown, GA. This was a small church with a family loving atmosphere, I begin to attend services regularly but I would always sit in the back. One Sunday morning while my dad was visiting me, I decided to ask him to go to church with me at City of Life Ministries in Grovetown GA. I was angry, hurt, bitter, and in a consistent argument with EJ that morning. We argued as I walked out the door. I eventually jumped in the car with my dad, rolled down the window, and started to curse EJ out good while heading out the drive way. I knew he couldn't put his hands on me while I was driving away, so I gave him my very best cursing speech, and it felt so good. I drove away laughing. My dad said, "You know you have to come back home right."

I laughed and said, "I don't care. He's not going to hit me if you're around, and after cursing him out good I'm still going to church."

Despite my behavior, I went to church, and on this particular Sunday, June 27, 2010. As messed up as I was, I walked in that church with my father and sat in the very back. On that day, I had the same mindset that I had at the mega church. I thought no one could really see me. No one could see I'm hurting. I told myself, I'm invisible. When I walked in the church, there was this small man with army pants on preaching. The members told me he was a Prophet. I noticed the whole time this man preached it seemed like he was looking at me, and I'm way in the back. I didn't care for it much but the words that were coming out of his mouth would hit me strong. When it was time for altar call, I felt like I should have gone up for prayer. I felt shame and I was being stubborn, so I didn't move when he asked people to come. I felt like I glued my feet to that floor, but then my dad asked me to let him by, and he went up for prayer. I knew I wanted prayer, I needed prayer but I refused to go. Then something said go support your dad. My dad is my heart and I thought it was a beautiful thing that he was getting saved. So I went and stood behind him to hide, but support him at the same time. The man of God prayed for him and then asked me to come from behind him. He prayed for me and I felt fire all over my body. I began to speak in a language I had never spoke in, and I couldn't stop crying and I couldn't stop shaking. I found myself on the floor in a fetal position, as if I was a baby again, and he kept calling me an intercessor. I recognized something was changing in me. This was the first time I went into a church and left a different way. I felt as if the shame, guilt, embarrassment, disgust, anger and bitterness had left me. My load became lighter the longer I stayed on that floor speaking in this unknown tongue with tears streaming down my face. I'm sure I could have filled up a bucket with all the tears I cried. My nose continuously ran, but I didn't care about how I looked. There was a warm fire of liquid love that I had never felt before consuming me. On that day, I knew something in me changed, I had a new birthday.

Hebrews 12:29 Our God is a consuming fire. (KJV)

John 3:5-7 Jesus answered, I assure you, most solemnly I tell you, unless a man is born of water and [even] the Spirit, he cannot [ever] enter the kingdom of God. What is born of [from] the flesh is flesh [of the physical is physical]; and what is born of the Spirit is spirit. Marvel not [do not be surprised, astonished] at My telling you, You must all be born anew (from above) (AMP)

"You are worth the sacrifice. Your debt has been paid. Don't create a new one".

Prayer: Heavenly Father, thank you for loving me enough to send Jesus to die for me. Thank you, Father for giving me the gift of your precious Holy Spirit. Thank you for loving me in spite of my sin. Forgive me for living a life that was unpleasing to you. Let your spirit fill me up from the inside out until I overflow. I want to be full of you and not of myself. I've purposely done things thinking I was proving a point, but in reality, I was just hurting myself more. Father allow your Holy Spirit to consume me and cleanse me. My spirit needs to be washed and cleansed because it is filthy from the sin, I committed by submitting myself to the world. I now submit myself to you.

Confession: *Jesus allow your love to flow through me. Holy Spirit, I am your vessel to use. I give you full permission to have your way in me. I have allowed myself to be used by people, and led by other spirits such as depression, anxiety, and low self-esteem. Today and from this moment forth, let me be filled and used by you. I know you love me the way I am, and you are the one to help me become who you called me to be. I submit to the voice and the power of the precious Holy Spirit. I am not who or what others labeled me as, I am not who the enemy said I am, I am strong, I am independent but dependent on God. I'm a broken individual with a strong God who has delivered me.*

*In this present moment, how do you feel about yourself? What do you think about yourself?

*When was the last time you attended church? If not recent, why?

Reflection:

Chapter 2 ~ Painful Transition

I've always been supernaturally gifted. After that Sunday, everything in my life changed quickly. My dreams and visions increased after my encounter with the Holy Spirit. When I was young, I would see demons and angels, I would hear voices call my name, and sometimes talk to spirits. I had numerous dreams about Jesus. As a young girl, I didn't understand what was going on with me. I thought I was normal. It wasn't until my brothers started asking my mom questions, like why do Lakeia always talk about seeing things, that I realized my gift.

I found myself knowing things before it happened, and when other kids witnessed what I spoke would come to past, they began to call me a psychic and I hated being called a psychic. I realized I was weird and different. I would have such heavy dreams about different spirits, and the future, that I would wake up screaming and my mom would have to hold me and pray with me. My mother knew there was something different about me. She would say I was special. After a prophet confirmed to her I was gifted, and had healing hands, my mother would take me to hospitals and people's houses to pray for them and they would be healed. Again, I was a young girl that did not understand what was going on with me, however I knew that I was supernaturally gifted. Because I was young and ignorant, I didn't understand the importance of my gift and I despised it because I felt like an oddball. I stopped telling people things I knew before it would happen, and I stopped telling anyone about my visions and dreams except my mom.

After being filled with the Holy Spirit, I told the Lord I wanted to serve him fully and if my relationship would continue to hinder my walk with him then I didn't want it. But I confessed to him that although my husband cheated so many times, I would not leave him unless I knew the woman he cheated with and could prove it. In July, God responded to my prayers. I found out EJ had slept with my best friend in my bed. It broke my heart. Not because I knew he cheated, I was use to him doing that, but because he cheated with her. I did not expect my best friend since the seventh grade to be the one my husband had slept with.

They asked how I found out. Well, my grandmother first mentioned it to me because it was something that had happened to my Godmother also. Then my mom called me on a Sunday morning and said I needed to pray and ask God if EJ slept with my best friend. I prayed, and I heard the spirit say "Yes". I asked my friend what happened and how it happened. She would not tell me. I prayed, and the Holy Spirit played everything before my eyes like a movie. I told her everything that happened, step by step. I told her how I saw her go in my master bathroom shower, get out naked while he laid on the bed, and she got on top of him and proceeded to have sex. She confirmed everything I said was correct. I was in shock for about three days. I had no emotions, I ate, worked, cleaned, and went on like nothing really happened. By the third day, something in me broke, I cried, yelled, screamed, and wanted to kill both of them. I started having heavy anxiety attacks, I could barely speak without crying. I felt alone, betrayed, lost, broken, wounded, angry, fearful, bitter, and confused. I could not understand how love could hurt so badly. No one ever told me about this pain, no one told me a pain like this could exist. I was so wounded; I couldn't do my day to day activities anymore without a huge breakdown.

After a few days, my best friend moved away from Georgia going back to North Carolina. Within a few weeks, I filed the papers to divorce EJ. Eventually, my mother came to Augusta and took me to the doctor. They wanted to admit me into a mental institution. My mom told the doctor to let her take me for a few months. I took leave from work and went with my mom to Cartersville Georgia, totally broken.

Psalms 51:17 *My sacrifice [the sacrifice acceptable] to God is a broken spirit; a broken and a contrite heart [broken down* *with sorrow for sin and humbly and thoroughly penitent], such, O God, You will not despise (AMP).*

When I arrived at my mom's home, I felt as if I was in a really dark place, but then somehow, light appeared. Mom would encourage me and pray with me. Every day she went to work, I found myself praying and crying out to God. My mother introduced me to different people that needed prayer and would push me to pray for them. She forced me to stir up the prophetic gift in me even in brokenness. As I operated in the spirit, I was reminded that this was the same thing she did to me when I was young, she would force me to use my gifts, even though I didn't want to. She always knew how to cultivate. And yes, I said force because I wanted to wallow in my misery. I wanted to just hurt and be depressed. I was in a "woe is me" state of mind, but my mother refused to allow my mind to stay there. I found the more I ministered to others, the more I prayed, the more I prophesied, the stronger I felt. I heard the Holy Spirit so clear. I thought it was so amazing that as broken and messed up I was, the Holy Spirit was using me on a level I had never imagined or seen.

Isaiah 57:15 *For thus says the high and lofty One -- "He Who inhabits eternity, Whose name is Holy: I dwell in the high and holy place, but with him also who is of a thoroughly penitent and humble spirit, to revive the spirit of the humble and to* *revive the heart of the thoroughly penitent [bruised with sorrow for sin](AMP).*

This is where I began to understand that God can use you in your brokenness. He receives and loves when you are broken because then he can actually begin to work with you and through you. When we are in a state of brokenness, we do not have the strength to do much, or to fight against his will, and this lack of strength allows the Father to work in your life. It allows one to see that it's not by your strength but by his, and while he's using you to minister to others, he's also healing you. Once I came to this revelation, I learned how to trust the Father.

Prayer: *Father, in the matchless name of Jesus, I repent of my sins. Father, I believe you sent Jesus your only son to die on the cross for me. I ask that you come into my life and take control. I ask that you fill me with your precious Holy Spirit. Father, I have encountered many painful trials, and I need help with forgiving myself, and forgiving those who hurt me. Father, I know I could not have made it this far on my own, so I thank you for covering me and keeping me. Holy Spirit, I ask that you help me to see myself the way you see me, and break all shame, guilt, bitterness, anger, hate, doubt, and insecurities off of me. I know you love me, and I surrender myself to you to do complete open-heart surgery on me. I am the clay and Father, you are the potter. Please do as you will with me in Jesus' name, amen.*

Confession: *God loves me. Although I am strong, it is ok for me to be weak in Jesus. When I am weak that is when he is strong. I do not have to carry the emotional and spiritual weight from my past or present alone. It is ok for me to cry because it is a natural and spiritual way of cleansing to my soul. I can do all things through Christ who strengthens me. I will not be afraid to forgive others or myself. I love me and it's ok to love me. As I continue to love me and encourage myself with the word of God, I can help strengthen others. I understand that if I am not healthy emotionally, spiritually, and physically, I cannot help anyone else. It's ok for me to heal and be selfish in this present moment so I can give freely and holistically to others later. I will not walk around in guilt or shame for loving me the way God loves me.*

"Brokenness does not mean weakness, it's a place of rebirthing. As a mother's water breaks before birth, God allows a breaking before rebirth."

*Who do you need to forgive? Will you choose to forgive them and yourself?

*What hurt are you emotionally holding on to that you need to confess and release to God?

Reflection:_____

Lakeia M. Smith

Chapter 3 ~ Broken

During my broken state, as I slowly healed, I would reflect on the past four years of my life. I thought about how insecure I had become over time because of the things EJ would do to me and say to me. I thought about all the women that I had encountered and how they despised me because EJ would be with them without my knowledge, and they wanted me out of the way. I thought about how I worked the entire time, how I stressed and did everything I could to provide for my family because he couldn't provide because of his criminal background, and his consistent encounters with law enforcement.

During the divorce process I was afraid. Afraid of him and what he would possibly do to me. He'd previously made threats saying he would have other women to jump me in the streets; he would drug me and take my son and other horrible things. He did mean things such as calling the light company and scheduled to have my lights turned off on my birthday, December 22, knowing it was winter. I happened to find out because I received a call from my father stating my lights were out. I knew this was not because of the bill because I always paid my bills on time. I called the light company and asked what happened, and the representative informed me that my husband called and scheduled the lights to be turned off on that particular day, my birthday, and if I didn't make it to the company to pay another deposit and fill out paperwork, then me and my son would be in the dark until after Christmas. This broke my heart. I remember crying so hard I could barely catch my breath because I couldn't understand how someone could be so devious. I had to leave work, and drive 45 minutes to get to the light company to have my lights restored or my family would have been in the cold for almost a week.

While going through all of this horror - the divorce, dealing with the betrayal, and feeling so heart broken, I continued to go to church and started going to a youth bible study at the Prophet's house, hoping to learn more about Christ and hoping to heal. At the bible study I met a young man who was a gospel rapper. For privacy purposes, we will call him Dee. I was intrigued by how well he knew the scriptures. He could quote scripture after scripture. Dee knew the exact book, chapter, and verse of everything we talked about. I felt acquired because I never quoted scripture like that; I was actually just learning them. I thought it was so cool how he would rap entire scriptures. For me this was an excellent way to remember them. One day he asked me to give him a ride home, and from that moment we became friends.

2 Corinthians 11:14 *And no marvel, for Satan himself is transformed into an angel of light (KJV).*

Still broken, still going through a nasty divorce, I chose to become really good friends with this guy. It seemed as if we were perfect friends. He had needs that I could help with like needing a ride to an interview, and I needed help with the scriptures. He talked to me about baptism. I knew somewhat of what it represented but he challenged me to study on it and encouraged me to get baptized. We became best of friends, traveling together, shopping together, going to the beach, just hanging out and having fun. We would pray together, fast together, and go to different church services together. He would support me in singing praise and worship, and I would support him in his gospel rap. Things seemed so perfect, but I still was broken, hurt, still wounded, and this guy seemed to have come at the right time in my life and helped me with my wounds. I felt free around him, I felt as if I could talk about anything, and slowly but surely, we formed a relationship, and fell into our lustful desires.

We dated for about a year and a half, and during that dating period some people agreed, some didn't. I had prophets, pastors, and different ministers to come and say this is your husband, and then I had others to say this is not your husband. It was all so confusing to me. I was a new babe in the spirit, and I was trying to hear God for myself, but that was hard because I had already encountered fornication before marriage.

I didn't want to keep hurting God, and I wanted to do the right thing, so Dee and I started planning a wedding a year after my divorce from my first husband. I never really allowed myself to heal, I never gave myself the opportunity to get to know me, so I met him broken, and married him broken because I allowed myself to fall victim to lustful desires. I had many people to come before the wedding took place and say that I shouldn't marry him. I prayed about it and asked God to stop the wedding if it was not his will. Dee ended up failing a drug test. He was on probation at the time for something he did in the early 2000s. His probation officer stated that he would have to turn himself in to go to jail. When I found this out, I cancelled the wedding a week before it was to take place. I took him to turn himself in and when we arrived at the jailhouse, they said there was no warrant for him and that he was good to go. Little did I recognize that it was a trap of the enemy.

When we found out he didn't have to go to jail, at that moment, we took it as a sign that maybe this is supposed to happen, so we called the wedding back on. This alone was a big sign and showed a lot of confusion, I did not recognize it then, but God was not in it because he is not an author of confusion.

1 Corinthians 14:33 *For God is not the author of confusion, but of peace, as in all churches of the saints (KJV).*

I continued on, still broken, still lost but thinking I was doing right, thinking I found the way, thinking I was healed. Dee and I married, and when we went on our honeymoon to the beach, we both cried, I felt like I had made the biggest mistake of my life for the second time around. He confessed to me that he still would have to go to jail when we returned home, and he cried about it. He confessed that he didn't' tell me because he knew if he did then I would not have married him, and he was right. I beat myself up, I thought I'd have to suffer whatever consequences that come with this because I was disobedient. There was no walking out, no turning back, and whatever healing I needed, I knew that I would have to try and find it by myself in Jesus; hoping the Lord would forgive me again.

1 John 1:9 If we confess our sins, he is faithful and just and will forgive us our sins and purify us from all unrighteousness (NIV).

I'm traveling down a new road, am I ready? Is the question I would ask myself, and then realize that it doesn't matter if I was ready or not, I had already taken the steps by saying "I Do". The journey had begun.

After shedding so many tears on our honeymoon at the beach, we decided to cut it short and return home. Dee went to jail upon our return home to Augusta. He called me every day crying, and asking me if God said anything because he needed about $2700 or he would have to do a little over 60 days. I told him, "You will be out soon. God will provide the finances."

I had $1200 from title pawning my car I had just paid off, and my spiritual sister loaned us the other $1500 just to get him out of jail. The painful part about this situation is when he was released, he did not show any appreciation. He treated me as if he used me. All the crying and pleading that he did in jail immediately disappeared. I was now $2700 in debt because of him, and the friend that I knew, the friend I had fell in love with, the friend that prayed and fasted with me, slowly disappeared before my eyes.

As time continued on, pressure and stress continued to build on me. We moved out of our home because we could not afford it. The financial stress really pressed on me because he did not want to work. He would start a job and not keep it for more than a month. We married May 5, 2012, by July 2012 we moved out our house and moved in with my Apostle, and on Sept. 10, 2012, my life changed.

The stress from the marriage, finances, and my job took a toll on me, everything seemed to have fallen downhill quickly after I married this man. I remember leading worship at the church anniversary on Sept. 9, 2012. While singing I felt a tingling sensation on the left side of my body. I had a horrible migraine, and the left side of my body became weak until I almost collapse. I was leading "Break Every Chain" by Tasha Cobb, and when I sung there is power in the name of Jesus, I retained some of my strength. While singing I was also praying. After service was over, I told Dee what happened, my head hurt extremely bad and the left side of my body was weak and continued to have a tingling feeling in my legs and arms. I went home and went to bed immediately thinking maybe if I get some sleep, I will be ok. I got up the next morning, and went to work, I still had a tingling sensation on the left side of my body and the horrible migraine. I remember sitting at my desk and my left leg and arm started to shake, still not knowing what was going on with me. I decided to take lunch and visit a friend. I thought that taking a walk might help with what I was physically feeling and talking with a friend would get my mind off of the pain. When I walked in the building where my friend's desk was located, I collapsed right in front of her. My body jerked as if I was having a seizure. I remember hearing people yelling all around me. The good thing is I worked at the hospital, so they easily transported me to the emergency room when the seizure was over.

Once they transported me to the emergency room, the nurses undressed me. The left side of my body continued to have slight jerking and tremors, and my speech had changed. I could not get any words out of my mouth without stuttering tremendously, although the words in my head sounded perfect. I remember the doctors asking me how I felt, and I would say, "I'm ok, I want to go home."

The doctor's response was, "Lakeia, we cannot allow you to go home until we find out what's wrong with you," He said, "You can't walk."

When he said I couldn't walk I looked at him with confusion thinking to myself, I've been walking fine, how does he think I made it to work, so I responded, "Yes I Can."

The doctor looked at me and said "Lakeia if you can walk, I will let you go home."

I said "O.K." I sat up on the bed with Dee assisting me. I placed my right leg down first and the strength in it was fine, but when I placed my left foot on the floor to stand up straight, I collapsed.

The doctor said, "See, we have to find out what happened."

I burst into tears. I literally could not walk. I had no strength in my left leg, my left arm would not stop jerking, and my speech was slow with a horrible stutter. What happened to me is all I could think, and why would this happen to me? My mother and brothers came to the hospital. I could see my brothers through the glass door standing outside crying and my mother telling them to be strong. Everyone was so upset, and I/we had no answers as to what happened to me.

The doctors ran all types of test on me. They collected several tubes of blood, did an MRI, and a CT scan and said they could not find anything. I continued to have seizures, I had about 15 one night at University Hospital, and the doctors had no idea as to what was going on with me. Eventually, they sent me to MCG - Medical College of Georgia Department of Neurology. I can honestly say I don't remember when they transported me over, I just remember waking up in a different hospital. However, as soon as I was admitted to my room, the nurses and doctors ran test. They took more blood, and an EEG, they questioned my mom about my life. The doctors asked me questions but barely being able to speak I could not respond much. It seemed I had a stroke, and I was epileptic, but once all the test results came back, they said there was no brain damage at all. The doctors ruled that I was not having real seizures, but I was having all of the symptoms, this led to their diagnoses, Migraines, Pseudoseizures and Conversion Disorder.

Migraine is a primary headache disorder characterized by recurrent headaches that are moderate to severe. Typically, the headaches affect one half of the head, are pulsating in nature, and last from two to 72 hours (https://en.wikipedia.org/wiki/Migraine 010120)

Psychogenic nonepileptic seizures (PNES), or pseudo seizures are paroxysmal episodes that resemble and are often misdiagnosed as epileptic seizures; however, PNES are psychological (i.e., emotional, stress-related) in origin. (http://emedicine.medscape.com/article/1184694-overview 010120)

Conversion disorder *is a mental condition in which a person has blindness, paralysis, or other nervous system (neurologic) symptoms that cannot be explained by medical evaluation. (https://medlineplus.gov/ency/article/000954.htm 010120)*

    My family and I did not believe this diagnosis. We were concerned that there was something else wrong with me; all of this could not have actually come from stress. My mother decided to take me home with her, so Dee, my son, and I packed up and moved to Cartersville. My mom set up appointments with psychologist, psychiatrist, neurologist, and the family medical doctor. More test were run on me. My neurologist found swelling around my brain and treated me for the inflammation and migraines, unfortunately the medication was so strong that it ate the lining of my stomach which caused me severe pain.

    The psychiatrist decided to place me on medication. I was prescribed several medications for my emotions. I was taking a total of seven different pills several times a day. The medicines included Xanax, Zyprexa, Topamax, Magnesium, Ibuprofen, Promethazine, and Benadryl. All of these medications, to help deal with the pain and burning in my head, the tremors and jerking, the seizures, and to help me rest. This was hard for me to deal with. I was 24 years old and felt like my life was taken from me. I had to have assistance washing, walking, be reminded to take my medication because my memory was affected by the medication, I couldn't speak for myself, couldn't drive anymore; I felt totally useless. I became severely depressed.

None of this made sense, and then I thought to myself, this is what happens when you are disobedient, so I deserve this. I began to over-eat. I would stay in my room in the dark, my mom would have to come get me to make me sit out in the living room with the family. I tried to pray and couldn't, I tried to read the bible but didn't understand anything I was reading. I felt like a total reject. I started to hate myself for my choices; I hated myself for taking my family through all of this pain, especially my mom. She would take me to my doctor appointments, make sure I took my medicine, help me wash, and pay my medical bills. Although I couldn't say anything, I knew in my mind that this was taking a toll on her and she was being affected by it.

Why? Over and over again I would ask myself. I thought, will I be like this the rest of my life? How is this affecting my son, seeing the condition I'm in? I cried many nights about my condition and the pain I was taking my son and my family through. I began to despise Dee because, he could not help take care of me, he couldn't provide for me, and he did not want to get a job no matter how much someone tried to talk him into getting one.

My life felt like it was crumbling second by second, minute by minute, hour by hour, day by day, week by week, month by month. I felt like a zombie because of the medicines I was taking. I did not have my own train of thought. If someone told me the sky was orange, I would just repeat that the sky was orange although I knew deep inside it was blue. I felt like I had no control over anything, and I was so used to being in control of my life decisions, finances, and activities, and all of that was so quickly snatched out of my hand. Church members would call and pray with me daily, to encourage me and express the love of Christ.

Although I know these people cared for me sometimes, I felt so horrible that I didn't want to talk to them. I was not allowed to go anywhere without assistance because I never knew when I would have a seizure. I had to be pushed in a wheelchair and carried a bag of medication with me everywhere I went. My mother was forced to consistently take time off work because I had several doctors' appointments each week, and my condition would not allow me to speak, understand, or drive. My mother realized she needed help with me, and the help would have to be someone she trusted. My loving cousin but more like a sister Timiya Floyd came all the way from Fairmont, NC to help me.

My mother definitely chose the right person to help me because she was a bodyguard, nurse, cousin, friend, and my sister. I love Timiya dearly, always have. I thought it was quite funny because when she was a little girl, I used to take care of her, and now here we are adults and she is taking care of me. She would not let people argue around me, or make me upset, she would not let me walk much, and if I did anything, I wasn't supposed to, she would tell. She was such a major blessing to me. However, with all the love and support I was getting from family and friends, I still felt like a burden. I still was in pain, my head would feel as if it was on fire, my mom would have to squeeze it to help relieve the pain, I had sharp pains in my head, along with the tremors and no strength on the entire left side of my body. My brain still had inflammation around it, and I was given medication to help bring the inflammation down, but yet I still would scream late at night from the excruciating pain. I was so tired and stressed, depressed, and broken. I thought what worst could possibly happen to me.

Prayer: *Heavenly Father I'm hurting, and I feel lost within myself. My thoughts are not like your thought. I know I'm supposed to think on those things which are good. I need your help; I'm confused and don't know why I'm suffering this way. I admit I was disobedient in many areas of my life and I repent. Proverbs 23:7 "For as he thinketh in his heart, so is he". Right now, all I can think about is my pain. You are my source of healing, you are my present help in the time of trouble, you are everything I need. I want to be made over by you. Help me heavenly Father, I know I can't get through anything without your precious Holy Spirit.*

Confession: *I command all spirits of fear, anger, depression, discouragement, and stubbornness to come out of me in the name of Jesus. Yea though I walk through the valley of the shadow of death, I will fear no evil, for God is with me. His rod and his staff comfort me. I pull down every stronghold that is trying to keep me bound and I cast down every imagination and every high thing that exalts itself against the knowledge of God, and I command my thoughts to become captive unto the obedience of God.*

Pain pressures you into your purpose and your purpose is God's plan - you are pressed into His will

When you continue to think on a situation over and over throughout your day, it is considered worrying. What are you spending most of your time thinking about?

Reflection:

Lakeia M. Smith

Chapter 4 ~ Fighting for Life

The Suicide Battle

One night after dinner, I started having heavy suicidal thoughts. I felt that things would be easier for everyone without me being around and being in the way. I thought my son would be happier not seeing his mom in a horrible condition, I thought it would be easier on my mom being that she was the one taking care of me, and as for Dee, he wouldn't care because he needed me to take care of him, and now that I couldn't, it wouldn't matter if I am here or not. I decided to grab one bottle of my pills and I slowly made my way to the bathroom. I didn't tell anyone, I just made the decision that I was going to take them all at one time and die because it would be easier for me and everyone around me. After I locked the door, I opened the bottle of pills and as soon as I turned the bottle up to throw the pills in my mouth, I heard a loud voice scream, "Shante' where are you?" The voice scared me so bad my body became hot and I broke out in sweats and replied back, "I'm in the bathroom".

It was my mom, she saved me, but she didn't know it. I hurried and put the medication away, and opened the door, but the weird thing is she didn't want anything from me. I sat and thought about what had just happened to me, what was I about to do, and why did she happen to scream my name at that exact moment. All of the sudden it hit me. The Holy Spirit spoke through my mom to yell at me at that exact moment to stop me from taking my own life. I realized God still had his eyes on me even in my moment of despair.

It reminded me of Adam and Eve in the garden when they ate the forbidden fruit. God cried out, "Adam where art thou?" Not that he didn't know where he was physically but there was a spiritual disconnection that happened when sin took place. I felt as if I was doing the same thing Adam and Eve did. That's the moment I realized God was a true father. I cried and repented. I asked the Father to forgive me, and Jesus to come and lead my life again. I told the Lord I will surrender completely and serve him, and I give all the gifts he gave to me back to him. Also I asked if he would heal me that I could dance again, I would dance, if he would allow me to speak again, I would speak whatever he tells me to speak, if he would allow me to lift my hands in worship again, I would praise and worship him in spirit and truth. If he would allow me to run again, I would run and jump and give him all the glory while doing it and not care what people would have to say. I re-dedicated my life back to Christ completely.

I realized that I had only given him part of me and because I never let him all the way in, he could not use me and speak to me as he desired to because I kept resisting him, and he is a gentleman, so he forces himself on no one.

Jeremiah 3:14 *Turn, O backsliding children, saith the LORD; for I am married unto you: and I will take you one of a city, and two of a family, and I will bring you to Zion (KJV).*

Proverbs 24:16 *For a just man falleth seven times, and riseth up again: but the wicked shall fall into mischief (KJV).*

As days went by, I would attempt to read my bible again. Little by little, I began to understand the word again, it came back to life in my spirit, and I received what I was reading. I fell down on my knees early one morning while my mom was gone to work. I asked the Holy Spirit to heal me and make me whole. I told him I would work for him completely, and I would give my testimony of what he has done for me. I immediately heard the audible voice of the Lord, and he gave me specific instructions as to how he was going to restore my strength.

Sometimes our Heavenly Father will give us instructions to see how obedient we will be for our own healing. People seem to think that God will just send a miracle out the sky just because you ask and just because that is how you want the miracle to be done. This reminds me of 2 Kings Chapter 5. In the bible there was a man named Naaman, a captain, a great and honorable man. Naaman wanted to be healed of leprosy but did not want to do what the Prophet Elisha told him to do by going to wash in the Jordan River seven times. The Jordan River was one of the filthiest rivers. Naaman felt that Elisha should have called on the Lord and laid his hands over the effected wounded places on his body to heal him. What we have to understand is God does not always work the way we think he should. His thoughts are greater than our thoughts and his ways are greater than our ways. Sometimes it's just our obedience that causes us to get our breakthrough and healing. Samuel told Saul obedience is better than sacrifice. I decided to obey God for my healing.

As the Holy Spirit spoke to me, I wrote down the instructions I heard. He said for me to take communion every day for thirty days. Every day I took communion, I would pray and spend time with him. I studied the word and began to confess the healing scriptures of the Lord over my body, mind and spirit. I did this routine the same time every day, and each day I felt stronger. Every day I took communion, I found myself speaking better, walking better, thinking clearer. Each time I took communion, I gave thanks to the Lord and I meditated on Jesus according to his word.

__1 Corinthians 11:24-26__ states, [24] and when he had given thanks, he broke it and said, "This is my body, which is for you; do this in remembrance of me." [25] In the same way, after supper he took the cup, saying, "This cup is the new covenant in my blood; do this, whenever you drink it, in remembrance of me." ²⁶ *For whenever you eat this bread and drink this cup, you proclaim the Lord's death until he comes (KJV).*

After the thirty days, I went from not being able to speak without stuttering to completing paragraphs. I went from being pushed around in a wheelchair due to having multiple seizures, to not having seizures at all and walking with a walker. By this time, my husband had left me and my son, went back to Augusta and gotten involved with another woman. I remember coming from church one day with my mom, and I felt a strong knot in my stomach as if I got punched. I heard the spirit say, he just cheated. I immediately texted him and asked him did he just cheat on me. Being who he was and wanting to hurt me, he told me, yes. He was with a young woman, who took off her clothes and became completely naked in front of him. He claimed he did not have full sexual intercourse with her. Again, I found myself hurt and broken. I prayed and wanted to go to Augusta right away. Not to mention, I was feeling pressure from my job saying if I didn't hurry and come back, then I would lose my position. I had been out of work for three months on medical leave and I was blessed they held my position for that long. The pressure from my job and my relationship placed me in a contentious state of mind. Do I go to Augusta and get my husband back, and my job, or do I stay in Cartersville and continue to heal?

Prayer: *Our father, which art in heaven, hallowed be thy name thy kingdom come thy will be done on earth as it is in heaven. Father, I have fallen short of your glory many times and yet you still love me. Father, help me to see through your heavenly eyes the plans that you have for my life. Help me to not falter or go astray anymore, but give me the strength, the heart, and the mind to stay the Holy course you have commanded me to walk. Thank you for your love you give me every day. Father, lead my way and cover me with your grace and give me your Holy strength to sustain if my flesh pulls me to go astray. All power and authority belong to you. Thank you for loving me like you do. I desire to please you and do your will. So, help me in my areas of weakness, and strengthen my heart in mind for the journey ahead.*

Confession: I command all spirits of confusion, arrogance, discouragement, doublemindedness, rejection, low self-esteem, and perversion to come out in the name of Jesus. Jesus has paid my debt with his blood sacrifice. I denounce every door that I have opened to witchcraft, demons, and devils by disobedience and sin. I am wanted and loved by God. He desires me to live and not die. The Holy Spirit has gifted me and wants me to be prosperous as my soul prospers. I have purpose, I have a destiny, I will not take my life. I have not seen the great things that God has for me and I will not leave this earth until I have completed my assignment from heaven, and until I have walked into the full manifestation of my heavenly blessings that are being released to me even now.

Suicide is not an option; suicide is not the answer. You were predestined to be here. Your life is worth living, and the answers you need lie within you because Christ lives in you. You are the hidden treasure the world is waiting on.

*Have you had suicidal thoughts and even made a plan? If so why, do you feel this way?

*Are you being faced with a decision that you want the

Father's help with? If so, what is it?

National Suicide Contact: 1-800-273-8255

Reflection:_____
_____
_____
_____
_____
_____
_____
_____
_____

Lakeia M. Smith

Chapter 5 ~ Confused

I spoke with my mom about moving back to Augusta. She did not believe I needed to move back in my current condition. She felt I needed more time to heal, and that it would be dangerous for me to move back because Dee was not in a good mental, emotional or financial place to take care of me and my condition. A part of me felt what she was saying was the best advice, but another part of me felt driven to try and work my relationship out. Against my mother's will, I moved back to Augusta. When I first arrived in Augusta, I found that Dee was living with his grandmother. I did not want to live with his family and therefore eventually found a home for us to live in.

Although I was not completely in my full strength to work, I returned to my job and worked as much as I could. Every day I would go to work, I continue to battle within myself with my health. I started having severe headaches again. I lost all the strength on the left side of my body and began to have seizures again, too. The stress of working, trying to take care of my home alone, and dealing with my husband, took a very heavy toll on me in my weak health condition. There were times I would go to work and the stutter would be so bad, my patients would tell me I needed more help than they did. I admit this was very embarrassing and hurtful, but I had to work because there was no other income source my family had because Dee refused to work.

After three months I was forced to resign due to my health issues. Because no one was working in my household, there was no income, and no income meant bills could not be paid. Dee and I eventually moved out of our three bedroom and two baths home and moved in with his grandmother. During this time period, I found myself depressed and lonely. Dee was in his familiar neighborhood and would hang out with other females, smoking marijuana, and doing whatever he felt he wanted to do. No matter how much I would ask him to stop with the females, he would not. His response would be, "I'm going to do what I want to do, and I knew them before I knew you." These are not the words a wife wants to hear, especially one that has sacrificed so much because she wants her relationship. I eventually realized this relationship was not going to work. This man didn't want to work, didn't want to be married, and didn't care much about me and my medical condition or my son. I decided it was time for me to leave.

As I strategized to leave my husband and move back to Cartersville, I found myself extremely sick. I started vomiting several times a day, I was weak and barely had strength to walk. Finally, I went to the emergency room. They ran some tests on me, including a pregnancy test. To my surprise, I was pregnant. I remember sitting there in the chair in a daze and in shock. The nurse called my name several times before I finally answered, and she asked was I okay. I thought to myself if you only knew my situation. I am pregnant by a selfish man-child, refuses to work, gets high all day, and I was planning to leave him. I silently stood up from the chair and received my discharge papers from the nurse. With tears in my eyes, I walked away. The ride home with this news and this man I no longer wanted to be with was a long ride. He finally broke the silence and said, "I knew you was pregnant."

So many thoughts ran through my mind, good and bad thoughts. I asked myself, should I still stay, or should I go? I don't want a child with this man, but I don't believe in abortion. If I keep this child, this means this guy I no longer want, will be part of my life forever. Is there a way out of this, or am I stuck? I found myself crying and praying and asking God to help me. I finally decided to stay and try to work things out in hopes that maybe this child would make a difference and maybe Dee would change now that we have new responsibilities. Little did I know this was the beginning of some of the worst days in my life.

Psalm 38:9 *All my longings lie open before you, Lord; my sighing is not hidden from you (NIV).*

1 Peter 5:7 *Casting all your care upon him; for he careth for you (KJV).*

As time continued, I found that the hormones from the baby caused the migraines to decrease. I slowly gained strength in my body. Although I was pregnant, this was a great thing because I needed all the physical strength, I could get because of the challenges my husband was taking me through. Every day I would wake up, there was an argument. He did not want me to leave his grandmother's house and when I tried, he would curse me, yell in rage, and take my car. I eventually found out that at this point Dee was not only smoking marijuana, but also synthetic marijuana called Spice.

Over the next several months, I found myself going through consistent battles with him that was both physical and dangerous. Sometimes the arguments and the verbal, physical, and emotional abuse became so dangerous that I would sneak away when he slept to go to stay with my oldest brother for a few days and sometimes my mother in Cartersville. However, through all the pain I was going through as a pregnant mother in an abusive relationship, I found myself still going to church and leading praise and worship. I found myself still preaching the gospel, and I found myself still praying for other people. One would think that with the abusive challenges I faced in my marriage, I would not go to church, but I found safety when I was in the presence of God, and I found safety when I worshiped with my brothers and sisters in Christ.

Proverbs 11:14 *Where no counsel is, the people fall: but in the multitude of counselors there is safety (KJV).*

Hebrews 10:25 *Not forsaking the assembling of ourselves together, as the manner of some is; but exhorting one another: and so much the more, as ye see the day approaching (KJV).*

During the birth of my second child, I found myself in a similar situation. Dee was dealing with other women, and while I was in labor with his son, he was on the phone with one. I thought to myself, there is no way this is happening to me the same way it did the first time. I never thought in a million years that I would be reliving my past. So yes, twice I was in labor with the first born child and son of a man and twice the man was cheating during my labor and twice I found myself crying because of emotional pain and disbelief. Twice I found myself sad and alone, the word déjà vu could not give my situation any meaning. The worst part is during my labor. I constantly kept vomiting. My heart rate and the baby's heart rate started to drop. Dee nor any of our family was around. Everyone hand gone downstairs for food. I remember beginning to fade out, but I still could hear loud shouts as the nurse ran into my room and screamed, "Help, she's coding".

Next thing I know, I felt hands touching me and flipping my body in different ways. I don't know what the doctors and nurses did to me, but I was happy to hear the words, "They're stable."

By the time the doctors stabilized the baby and me, Dee and his family returned to my room. I told him what just happened to his son and I, and to my surprise he showed no care or concern. He was very nonchalant about the situation. I knew from that point on, I had to make some serious decisions concerning my life, my children's life and our safety.

A huge part of me wanted everyone to be happy and hoped that the baby would help bring change to my relationship, but that was not the case. After my son was born and we were discharged from the hospital, things became worse. Dee became more abusive physically, so much the cops were called numerous times. I found out later he was not just using synthetic marijuana but also cocaine. I recognized that his behavior became worse; he would act almost similar to a drunk man but did not smell like alcohol.

As time passed, I left to live with my mother for about a month to heal after having the baby. My husband would not allow me to rest, not help with the baby, and he was a danger to me, my children, and himself. After I retained my strength. I went back to Augusta with Dee. For about a week he was respectful and contained his negative behavior. I realized this was a cycle that was never going to end. He threatened to kill me numerous times if I left with his son, and he tried to set himself on fire in front of me. During this time of my life, I called out to God like never before, because I wanted out but didn't know how to get out. My mother would call and ask me why I am living like this, and the only answer I had for her is, Mom I can't leave him. I met a Caucasian lady that was part of a homeless organization and talked with her about my situation. I had no money, no job at the time, no car, but I wanted a place for me and my kids. I no longer wanted to live with Dee and his family. Dee saw me speaking with this Caucasian lady and walked up behind me as soon as she asked the question, do you want your husband to live with you. My heart was beating fast, my body became hot, inside I was screaming *no I don't*, but out of my mouth came the words, "Yes He Can Come".

Oh why, oh why, oh why, oh why, did you say that Lakeia? I felt like crying. I allowed the fear he had placed in me to control my way out; this is what I had prayed for, and this was my opportunity to step into freedom. I convinced myself that I made the right choice. I told myself if we had our own house and we were no longer living with his family, he would do better. I knew in my heart, this was not true, but I continue to force myself to believe this lie.

Psalms 69 *¹ Save me, O God, for the waters have come up to my neck. ² I sink in the miry depths, where there is no foothold. I have come into the deep waters; the floods engulf me. ³ I am worn out calling for help; my throat is parched. My eyes fail, looking for my God. ⁴ Those who hate me without* reason outnumber the hairs of my head; many are my enemies without cause, those who seek to destroy me. I am forced to restore what I did not steal. ⁵ You, God, know my folly; my guilt is not hidden from you (NIV).*

Prayer: *Heavenly Father, I have made many mistakes, and even when I try to do right, evil is always around me. I feel like Paul when he writes in Romans 7:19-25. "For I do not do the good I want to do, but the evil I do not want to do – this I keep on doing. ²⁰ Now if I do what I do not want to do, it is no longer I who do it, but it is sin living in me that does it."*

Father, help me with my sinful nature that I may be clean and not continue to live in negative cycles and continue bad habits. I desire to be Holy as you are Holy. Father, forgive me, and I forgive myself. I know you will uphold me, and I am slowly learning to seek you before making decisions for my life. I've realized the decisions that I make for myself are foolish but if I converse with your precious Holy Spirit before making decisions, I will never make the wrong decision. You are perfect in all of your ways Father, and you have never made a mistake and never will. Help me to be disciplined to study your word and spend more time with you so that I can have the mindset of Christ. I desire to renew my mind daily, thank you for loving me, keeping me, providing for me, and never giving up on me. I know that you are more than able to keep me from falling, and I make the decision to completely trust you, thank you for giving me another chance, in Jesus' name. Amen.

Love is not fear, but perfect love casteth out fear. If they really love you, you will not fear their presence. It's not true love if it's not like the love of God.

*Have you ever made the same mistake twice? If so, how do you feel about your decision?

*Do you feel that God is upset because you may have made the same mistake or because you made a new mistake? Do you believe he will forgive you again?

Reflection:_____
_____
_____
_____
_____
_____
_____
_____
_____
_____
_____
_____
_____
_____

Lakeia M. Smith

Chapter 6 ~ The Pressing of Faith Activated

I found myself in a very rough place. I had the opportunity to get a home for my family but in order to move into the home, I had to have a job. I had one month to sign papers and turn in proof of employment in order to move into my own home through the homeless organization program. I prayed and the Lord answered my prayers, I received a job offer just in time to move, and the offer letter was my ticket into my new home.

The next hurtle I had to overcome was transportation. My previous vehicles no longer worked, and I would pay to catch a ride to the places I needed to go. For about one month, I would either walk or catch a ride to work. By the time I received my second check, I prayed and asked God for help, and asked him to give me favor for a car.

During the one month I worked, I met another young woman who loved the Lord and stated to me her husband worked at a dealership and would love to help me. I was elated to hear such comforting words; I knew nothing was guaranteed but it was a start. I went to visit the dealership one day after work with only $300 in my pocket, this was all I had left after paying my bills. Dee at the time still did not work, was not looking for a job, and was still abusing drugs, therefore all of the financial burden was left on me. I coached myself into a mindset that I had to live as a single mother of two children and a grown child (my husband), and no matter what he did, I needed to make sure everything was taken care of for me and my children. As I approached the dealership, the salesman greeted me with a joyous smile. He took me into his office, and we discussed my options for a vehicle. I informed him, all I have is $300.00 and I believe that the Lord will take care of the rest. As he walked me through the purchasing process after reviewing my credit and income at that time, he stated I would need $1000.00 down, and my car payment would be between $255.00 to 350.00 a month. I responded to him saying I want a Honda, and I don't want my payments over $255.00 a month. He told me to think about it and let him know when I get the full $1000.00. I left the dealership and went home and prayed. I reminded the Father of his word, and this was my prayer:

Prayer: *Father, in the wonderful name of Jesus, the name above all other names. Daddy, in your word Jesus said in Matthew 6:26 Take no thought for my life, what shall I eat, drink or wear because father you take care of the fowls of the air and they sow not, and I am much better than they are (KJV). You said not to worry about tomorrow because tomorrow will take care of itself, but to seek ye first the kingdom of God and his righteousness, and all these things shall be added unto me. Father, I don't have all the money the dealership is asking for, but you do, and Paul said in Philippians 4:19 But my God shall supply all your need* *according to his riches in glory by Christ Jesus (KJV). So, I thank you for my new Honda, I thank you my payments are affordable for me to pay, I thank you for the money for the down payment. I thank you that your favor and your grace is more valuable than money. Daddy, you have never left me or forsaken me, and I know you will continue to take great care of me. By faith Father, I stepped out and went to the dealership because I need a vehicle. So, Father, I thank you for providing the vehicle that you want me to have, that is suitable for me and my children. I trust you, I adore you, I love you, and I know that I have what I need because I am a child of the King and according to Romans 8, I am a joint-heir and I have inherited the kingdom inheritance which means I don't have to want for anything. Thank you, daddy, for taking care of me, in Jesus' name. Amen.*

The next day after work I received a visit from a very close friend, and she stated to me the Lord told her to give me $200.00. I responded to her, "He told you to GIVE it to me?"

She looked at me with a huge smile and said, "Yes, he told me to bless you with this $200.00 and you do not have to pay it back." I gave God glory right away. I jumped, shouted, and shed a few tears of joy. My $300.00 had increased to $500.00 over night. My Father had begun to answer my prayers.

That same night, I received a call from the dealership, and my salesman said, "I don't know why I'm doing this, I don't know you at all personally, Ms. Lakeia, but if you have the $500.00, I will put the other $500.00 with yours so you will have the full $1000.00 to get your car, and you just pay me back when you get your income tax refund."

Immediately I broke, and really shouted then, because I know that was no one but my Heavenly Father that would allow such favor and blessings to reign over me, and not just reign over me but it was a 24 hour responsive blessing. Hallelujah.

Psalm 37:4-5 *Delight thyself also in the* LORD: *and he shall give thee the desires of thine heart.* ⁵ *Commit thy way unto the* LORD; *trust also in him; and he shall bring it to pass (KJV).*

I went to the car dealership the next day, and my salesman met me in the lot with a huge smile. As promised, he had the $500.00 cash, and I gave him my $500.00 cash. I signed papers on November 21, 2014 for a 2007 Honda Accord with payments at $254.00 per month. The car was spacious, didn't have many miles on it, and was perfect for me and my children. My heavenly Father answered my prayers and provided everything I needed. He responded to my faith, and he said all I needed was faith the size of a mustard seed.

After receiving my car, my job, and my home all within a three-month period, I was full of joy. My faith level was at an all-time high because I witnessed God moving things so quickly in my life. I realized how powerful praying was. I knew I always prayed, but I never prayed with such intensity, I never prayed with such great expectation, I never prayed with such faith. This process I was going through taught me so much about the power of prayer, that I began to study more about prayer, I began to fast more and asked God to show me more. My zeal for him had increased because I was a living witnessed that he didn't just work miracles, but he's still working miracles quickly.

As my relationship continue to grow with the Lord, my battle in my marital relationship increased. Just because God was working out all of my needs didn't mean Dee had stopped using drugs, had stopped using abusive words, had stopped trying to hurt himself, or had stopped being mean period. Every day I still had to deal with Dee and his aggressive ways. The fact God blessed me with a car caused more issues because he would take my car late at night and would go get high. He still refused to get a job, but he would tell me he needed to drop me off at work every day and drop the kids off at school and use the vehicle to find employment. I knew this was the trick of the enemy. I knew he was lying every time he made this statement because when I reached out throughout the day to check in, he would say something came up and he didn't have time to go look for a job.

The verbal, physical, spiritual, and emotional abuse became so bad, I would have both of my boys in the bed sleeping with me, lock the door, and slept with a knife under my pillow because I never knew when he was going to act out. I continued to cry out to God and ask him for a way out of this because it was not safe for me and my children. I still prayed for Dee that God would save, heal, and deliver him, and I even prayed saying Father if this is my fault, forgive me, and deliver me, and help me so my family can be whole. It seemed the more I prayed the worst he became. If he knew I was in the room praying he would scream, curse, yell, and would say negative things about me like "You're A Wife from Hell". If he knew I was resting with the children at 3 a.m. in the morning he would yell and curse, and I knew his behavior was so ruthless because he was high.

Although I was going through so much at home with Dee, I would not stop ministering the word of God. I continued to sing praise and worship, I continued to declare the word of God every time I was faced with an issue and when church members, family or friends called me with their issues I would give them the word of the Lord. I continued to encourage the people that no matter what we are dealing with, we must use the scripture to speak to our situation. This is the method Jesus used in *Matthew 4:4* when Satan came to tempt him, he stated *"It is written, man shall not live by bread alone, but by every word that proceedeth out of the mouth of God"*.

We must realize for every circumstance and challenge we face there's a scripture for it. I continued to apply this method to my life daily because in all that I was personally dealing with the word is all I had. The word is the only thing that kept and continues to keep me in my right mind. I knew focusing on the word of the Lord was a great thing, but I realized church folk became frustrated with me for giving them scriptures for their issues. They said things to me such as, why do you always answer with the word of God, why can't you be a normal person, or make statements as you live too Holy, and all you talk about is the scriptures when someone tell you there issues. I remember praying and crying after hearing those questions and comments, because it hurt me very deeply. I told God, *I don't understand, I thought we were supposed to speak your word to our circumstances and I thought we were supposed to trust you and pursue holiness, but people in the church are coming up against me for doing what I read you do in the bible.* I realized I'm not just battling at home but now I'm battling in the church as well. Jesus was all I had, focusing on him was my only hope.

I could not be moved by what people was saying about me. I knew the word of God is truth, and I had to follow truth. No, I did not think I was greater, holier, or better than anyone, I just knew the scriptures has the answers I need, and I knew the scriptures is what brings comfort in the time of trouble. When people called me for guidance, or because they were broken and wounded, all I could offer was prayer and comforting scriptures from the word of God.

I knew the word worked because it was working for me with all the hell I was experiencing at home. I understood people will talk about you whether you're doing good or bad, so never change to please others, but focus on pleasing God and everything will work out in your favor.

Dee finally decided to apply for a job after several months of doing nothing and was hired. The job was a very decent job, he could have made a good career working for one of the biggest hotel brands. However, he lost his job after one month of working because of his attitude. He continued to hang out late at night with females.

One night after reading my word, I went out the door at 11 p.m. on my porch looking for him. I found he was in between the house in the car in the dark with a girl, then jumped out the car, cursed me out and said I was interrupting them. The girl laughed in my face. I went back in the house and prayed. I eventually burst into tears; I just could not take it anymore.

The next day after work, I went over to the young woman house and told her to never step foot into my yard again. We argued and as I found myself about to hit her. I heard the Holy Spirit say, "If you get into a fight again, you will win but this time you will go to jail."

When I heard this in my spirit, I immediately stopped arguing with her and walked away. She thought I left because of her. No, I did not, but I had to let her think what she wanted. It was embarrassing but I didn't care because I know that when the Holy Spirit speaks, it's going to come to past. I was blessed he gave me warning that if I hit this girl, I would win but I would go to jail, and I was willing to be embarrassed vs. going to jail. I did not care what she thought of me after that.

Let me submit to you, the reason the Lord said, "This time you will go to jail." I'd previously been in several fights because of this man and other reasons and I won the physical fights but never went to jail. I fought because I had to, not because I wanted to, however, dealing with heavy warfare, both physically and spiritually, caused me to be angry. And yes, I still sung praise and worship, still prayed, and preached but at the same time found myself fist-fighting from time to time to protect myself and my children. I fought more in my twenties after getting over a heavy sickness than I had ever fought in my entire life.

Again, I continued to pray, because there was nothing else, I could do. If God didn't help me then no one could. In the home the Father had blessed me with filled with brand new furniture that I didn't' have to pay for, driving a car that I was favored to have, I became depressed. On the night of January 11, 2015, I entered into prayer and went to sleep. I dreamed and I saw myself on the floor singing:

Lord we have been broken misused,

Father we've done all we know to do
Lord we need a miracle from you,
Father we've done all we know to do
So, we cry out for a miracle, we cry out for your healing Lord
We cry out for a miracle from you

We need a miracle,
We need your healing Lord
We need a miracle from you
We need a miracle,
 We need your healing Lord
We need a miracle from you

After I worshipped in the dream, I shifted and saw myself on the floor praying and crying, leaning on a couch with my normal everyday clothes on. All of a sudden, the room I was in filled with a cloud of smoke, and it looked as if I was floating on clouds. Then I saw a bright glorious light and a man walked in the room with an all-white robe on and a gold sash around his waist, and across his shoulder. His face was full of peace, and he had long hair with a beard and the most gentle eyes of love, and I trembled and said to him, "I know who you are, you are the Lion of Judah, you are the Prince Of Peace, You are my Lord." He looked at me with a soft loving smile and said to me "Don't Be Afraid Of My Presence." Immediately, he wrapped his arms around me and hugged me tight. Black gunk rose from my feet and came all the way up to my head and covered my entire body. Then it broke and shattered off me like glass shatters. When I looked at myself, I no longer had on my regular clothes, I had on a white robe with a gold sash around my waist and shoulder just like he did, and then he disappeared.

Zechariah 3:3-4 *Now Joshua was dressed in filthy clothes as he stood before the angel.* ⁴ *The angel said to those who were standing before him, "Take off his filthy clothes". Then he said to Joshua, "See, I have taken away your sin, and I will put fine garments on you (KJV)."*

When I awoke the next morning, I felt joy and I wept with joy because I knew Jesus, (Yeshua) came and personally healed me, delivered me, and strengthened me for the battle that I was facing. I also emailed my praise and worship leader my song, "Miracle" and we began to sing it almost every Sunday. We were requested to sing the song at many different ministries, and every time the song was sung, deliverance took place. My heavenly father anointed the song he gave me and cleansed me all in one night. I have since recorded the song so that many other ministries could hear it and worship to it as well.

Confession: *I will not live in fear, my heavenly father watches over me and will always provide a way of escape. I will worship him and not worry, I will walk in faith and no longer fear, I will put on the garment of praise for the spirit of heaviness, I* *will love more. I choose to give God the very best of me and I know everything else is taken care of because Matthew 6:33 states "Seek ye first the kingdom of God and his righteousness and all these things shall be added unto me" (KJV). I make the decision to seek the Kings righteousness and his kingdom.*

Worship Shifts Worry
Faith Shifts Fear
Praise Shifts Pity
Love Shifts Low Self-Esteem
I Choose to Do the Latter

*What Miracle are you in need of?

*Are you willing to worship while you wait?

Reflection_____
_____
_____
_____
_____
_____
_____
_____
_____
_____
_____

Chapter 7 ~ It's Time to Fight Back

After my experience with Jesus, I felt renewed, revived, and strengthened. I woke up excited, and I found that the fear I had of my husband was no longer there. I recognized he did his normal morning behavior, waking up yelling, cursing and upset. However, no matter how much he acted out, it did not bother me. He wanted to keep my car like he normally did so he could run around town all day doing nothing while I was working and while my kids are at school. I told him, "NO, I'm driving to work, and I'm taking my boys to school".

I found out that day what the bible meant when the scripture reads in *Isaiah 54:17*, *No weapon that is formed against thee shall prosper (KJV),* because he yelled and cursed, and then he confessed something that I would have never thought I would hear an individual say. He looked at me with piercing red eyes and said, "YOU WERE NOT SUPPOSED TO MARRY ME, AND A WITCH CONFIRMED TO ME WHY I WAS SENT TO YOU, I WAS SENT TO DISTRACT YOU FROM YOUR DESTINY."

I sat quietly and stared at him; I could not believe the words that came out of his mouth. I thought about how quickly my life went downhill after I took a covenant with this man. Despite what my mom said, despite what my pastor said to me, I realize it was all a trick and the plan of the enemy to kill me.

John 10:10 *The thief cometh not, but for to steal, and to kill, and to destroy (KJV).*

I came to myself and I thanked the Father because he did not allow me to die in my mess. He did not allow me to die in my disobedience, he did not allow me to die even when the attack was so much greater than I felt I could bare, and I found that "Greater is he that is in me, than he that is in the world." This entire time, this man was being used to try and destroy me. After this awful confession from him, the warfare increased. He said things like, "I'm going to bring candles to channel angels and spirits in this house", and he would tell me things like "you are not to call on the name of Jesus in this house, because that is not his real name."

I found myself battling with him day after day concerning the name of Jesus. When he saw me praying, he would say, "Jesus is not his name," when he heard me worshiping, he would say, "Jesus is not his real name. You are being lied to in church." Day and night, he would tell me that I shouldn't' call on the name of Jesus. He said this so much to me, I found myself beginning to doubt.

One morning I prayed and said "Holy Spirit, please reveal the truth to me. I'm beginning to find myself confused, fighting this battle concerning calling the name of Jesus. Please confirm to me if I am right. After I prayed this prayer, the Holy Spirit took me to 2 *Timothy* 3. I read the entire chapter, and he highlighted verses 13-15 *But evil men and seducers shall wax worse and worse, deceiving, and being deceived. But continue thou in the things which thou hast learned and hast been assured of, knowing of whom thou hast learned them; And that from a child thou hast known the holy scriptures, which are able to make thee wise unto salvation through faith which is in Christ Jesus (KJV).*

After reading these scriptures and being led by the Holy Spirit, I was grounded in believing the name of Jesus has all power and no matter how much Dee would yell at me to stop calling on the name of Jesus, I refused to stop. In fact, I increased praying and calling the name Jesus all through my home.

I later found out a warlock was mentoring Dee. He dabbled in witchcraft and read many books outside of the bible. I continued to pray, and no matter, I still called on the name of Jesus, and I would say it loud. He would respond and tell me how much he hated me and didn't like me and didn't want me. I gained more compassion for him because I knew he needed Jesus more than anything, although he was now fighting against him. I found myself in a war with witchcraft in my home.

One night after praying before bed, I had another dream. In my dream, I was in a place that looked like a mountain of fire and lava. I was dressed with a helmet that allowed my hair to be pulled up in a ponytail and out of my face, I had a huge breast plate with a picture of the cross on my chest and it also covered my back. I had a belt around my waist, my shins where covered, and my feet was covered, I held a shield in my left hand, and in my right hand was a huge sword. The sword was ten times the size of a regular sword, and it had burning fire. The fire blazed brightly. It was red, yellow, and orange. Although the sword was huge, burned with fire, and should have been heavy for me, it did not burn me, and I was very comfortable holding it. My warrior armor-like outfit was stronger and better than Wonder Woman's. I found myself on this mountain of fire and lava, and demons heads kept popping up out the ground, and with my mighty sword, I would chop off their heads, and after killing numerous demons, I held the sword to the sky, standing in a position as to honor God. I woke up the next morning breathing heavy and excited, as if I had just come out of a war that was won.

 As I prepared for work, I noticed Dee was not bothered or upset. He'd cleaned the house, cooked breakfast, and was preparing dinner. I admit, I was very skeptical about eating the food, but I prayed and said Lord you brought me this far. If there is anything in here, I trust you got me because I know my time is not up yet. After work, I went to my prayer closet, and I asked the Father what steps I needed to take next. I really needed to hear from him because I knew I wouldn't make the best decisions without the leading of the Holy Spirit. During prayer, I heard the Holy Spirit say you are going to Africa, I replied Africa? An hour after I prayed, I received a call from my sons' godmother, and she said, "Lakeia, I am going to a prayer meeting tonight with the Africans and it was placed on my heart to ask you to come. The prayer meeting will take place in North Augusta, SC at an African braid shop and it will be from 11 p.m. – 4 a.m."

It was the weekend, so I didn't mind. My boys were with their grandmothers and Dee wanted me gone from the house anyway because he was smoking and had company. I took a nap and set my alarm to wake up at 10 p.m. When it was time to get up and get dressed, I jumped with excitement. I drove to the African braid shop, and when I arrived the people were praising the Lord.

The African people were amazing. they worshiped with nothing but their mouths, hands, and one drum. They would sing praises to the Father and they would march around in a circle clapping and praising. After they sung, they would pray. Different individuals would pray for the different issues the Holy Spirit placed on their hearts. For example, someone would jump up and pray for the children, another lady would jump up and pray for the men in the body of Christ, another lady would jump up and pray that Christian people would be delivered.

After several prayers, they would begin to praise again, they would worship and call God papa, they would march in their circle clapping their hands, stomping their feet praising the Lord. Then the man of God would stand up and the interpreter with him, and he would begin to minister the word of God powerfully, speaking in his native language while the interpreter would repeat in English. After he spoke the word of the Lord, the people would go back to praising and praying. This cycle went on for hours, prayer, praising, and word, prayer, praising and word. After several hours, when the Man of God spoke again, he began to prophesy. He looked at me and said, "You are a wealthy woman, you will write many books and you will write best sellers, and you will write in your book about this night when this little African Man, who couldn't speak English prophesied to you at this prayer meeting."

I looked at this man, and my first thought was he obviously don't have any idea of the hell I'm going through. The Lord could not have possibly told him to speak that word because I'm stuck in a horrible marriage, fighting witchcraft, and still trying to live for Christ and stay sane and the prophetic word I receive is about books. After he prophesied and they praised and prayed again, I closed my eyes and quoted *Mark 9:24*, "*Lord I believe but help my unbelief (KJV).*"

As time continued, my landlord came by my home and informed me the state decided to purchase the home that my family and I was in, and we had 15 days to move. I still didn't have any money and did not know where I was going to go. After being told this awful news, I decided not to fear, I went back to my prayer closet, I prayed a prayer I have never prayed before and talk to God in a way that I have never spoken to him before. The prayer I prayed goes as follows:

Prayer: *Father God, they said I have to move out of this house immediately and you know my financial situation, but I know that you always take care of your children. Daddy I want a 4-bedroom house, with 2 bathrooms, carpet all through the house, a big front yard, and a big back yard, in Jesus' name.*

Hebrews 4:16, *"Let us therefore come boldly unto the throne of grace, that we may obtain mercy, and find grace to help in time of need (KJV)."*

I got up off my knees and read my word. In less than an hour coming out of my prayer, I received a call from the same woman that told me I had to move. When I answered my phone, the first thing she said is "Lakeia, you must have someone working miracles for you. After delivering the news to you about relocating, I received a call from another woman with a 4-bedroom house, 2 bathrooms, carpet all through the house, and it has a big front yard, and back yard for your kids to play in. Also, you don't have to worry about a deposit or rent, you just need to have your utilities transferred, and you can move into the house this weekend." The entire time she was talking, I laughed hysterically because I knew what I just prayed. When the call ended, I jumped up and gave the Holy Ghost a big shout. Hallelujah, Thank You, Jesus!

2 Peter 1:3 *His divine power has given us everything we need for a godly life through our knowledge of him who called us by his own glory and goodness (NIV).*

After my family and I moved into our bigger home, the Father blessed us with, the Lord began to increase my dreams. He would tell me to stay home from work and pray different times of the month. During the days I stayed home praying, I would have heavenly visitations, open visions, and receive prophetic instructions concerning my life and the life of others. I would give Dee the warnings the Lord gave me for him, when he slept at night, as I sat up praying and meditating on the word, I saw the spirit of death over him twice. Although he was abusive and became dangerous for me and my children, I did not want him to die. I knew the relational love in our hearts was no longer there, the romance had died but I still did not want this man dead because he was the father of my child. After the spirit of death visited and I prayed and rebuked him, Dee had a breakdown.

On the way to taking my son to school one morning, he was driving, and he would swerve in and out of traffic quickly. It scared me and my son, so I spoke to him calmly and asked him to slow down. Once we arrived at my son's school and he safely went in, Dee pulled off dangerously. He drove more dangerously than before, and I screamed, "Slow down, slow down or I'm calling the police."

He responded, "Call them."

So, I did. I called 911 and told the lady we were driving down Gordon Highway going 80 miles per hour. Dee screamed out things like have you ever been on a high-speed chase and are you ready to go to heaven. The 911 operator heard everything he was saying and told me to stay on the phone with her and to ask Dee to take me home. He continued to scream at me, and I started praying. I told the operator the direction we were going and gave her my address. He finally calmed down and said I'm taking you home. When we arrived up at my home, the police were waiting for us. I jumped out of the car, and the officer walked up to me and asked me why you are still allowing yourself to go through this. You've had to call us several times concerning this man and you don't have to live like this. My response was, "Yes sir, you are right."

That morning, the suicidal crisis counselors came to our home and took him, and admitted him to the mental hospital in Savannah, Georgia. The hospital held him and refused to let him come home until I said I was safe. I could not say I felt safe, so he stayed until they felt the need to release him, but he was no longer allowed to come back to our home. He called me and let me know that he did not want me, he did not like me, and he stated to me, "You're stupid because I've given you many ways out of this relationship, but you refuse to leave."

I thought about it, and I said to myself, I cannot be angry with him. He's right. I refused to leave after being abused emotionally, spiritually, financially, and physically. I refused to leave because church folks said stay, but then his family would tell me to get out of this relationship. I refused to leave hoping things would change but it became more dangerous for me and my children each passing day. I refused to leave because I thought I deserved the abusive treatment because I married a man my parents and leaders in my life said not to and I didn't want to hear, "I told you so." I refused to leave because I convinced myself that he would love me again, and I loved him. But as I reflect on the years that had passed with the continual drug abuse, cheating, the lies that had been told, the verbal and physical abuse, the disrespect, the fear I had waking up every day wondering what would happen next, I realized this is not what God wants for me and this is not love according to the word of God. Dee wanted a divorce a long time ago, but I refused to let go. This last major incident happened in December of 2015. I made up my mind that I was done with this relationship, and I could not continue to live this way.

I focused more on myself, my children, but most of all my relationship with God. My prayer life increased because I allowed the distractions to decrease. As I drew near to the Holy Spirit, he drew near to me. I only wanted his voice, I only wanted to know what he wanted for me. By March of 2016 I received a vision that showed the next three things that would happen in my life. The first was a divorce, the second was to be ordained in the office of a prophet, and the third was relocation. Within two weeks, I received unction to start the divorce process. Of course, when certain Christians heard I was divorcing my second husband, they started to talk and say things to me such as the *Father don't like divorce*. They did not know that I'd done my research on biblical reasons for divorce and I was in alignment with the word. Adultery had already taken place and my unbelieving spouse declared he wanted to give me a written divorce.

1 Corinthians 7:15-17 But if the unbeliever leaves, let it be so. The brother or the sister is not bound in such circumstances; God has called us to live in peace. ¹⁶ How do you know, wife, whether you will save your husband? Or, how do you know, husband, whether you will save your wife (NIV)?

However, I did not feel the need to explain myself. I found out that when you are in alignment with God's will and when he tells you to do something, you do not have to defend yourself. He will fight the battle for you. **Psalms 46:10** *Be still and know that I am God (KJV).*

One night, an African Christian woman prayed for me after doing my hair. She said if it is the Father's will for this divorce to happen, then it will happen with ease and you will not have to fight or force the divorce process. Everything flowed so smoothly as soon as I started the process. A co-worker had introduced me to her lawyer friend who represented me at a very favorable and affordable price. Dee had a heart of sadness but did not put up a fight and signed the divorce papers. Within 45 days I was divorced.

***Prayer:* DELIVERANCE PRAYER FOR THOSE GOING THROUGH DIVORCE / BEEN DIVORCED**

Father, in the name of Jesus, I confess that you are Lord overall, both good and evil. Father, thank you for being Elohim, my God. Thank you for being Jehovah Jireh, the provider. Thank you for being Jehovah Rapha, the Lord who heals. Thank you for being Jehovah Nissi, Lord our banner. Thank you for being Jehovah M'kaddesh, the Lord who sanctifies. Thank you for being Jehovah Shalom, the Lord that is peace and gives his people peace. Thank you for being Jehovah Tsidkenu, our righteous God. Thank you for being Jehovah Rohi, my shepherd. Lord, the earth is yours and the fullness thereof; there is nothing that you can't do. Jesus, you are King of Kings. Lord, you spoke the world into existence, and it belongs to you. Thank you, Father. So today, Lord, I submit myself to you as a broken and wounded vessel and ask that you take control of my life.

Lord, your word said in James 5:16, "Confess your faults one to another, and pray one for another, that ye may be healed. The effectual fervent prayer of a righteous man availeth much" (KJV). So, I confess. Lord, I am hurt. I confess, Lord, I am broken. I confess, Lord, that I feel disappointed. I confess, Lord. that I am angry. I confess. Lord. that I am bitter. I confess, Lord, that I struggle with trust and insecurities in myself. I confess, Lord, that I am afraid. I confess, Lord, that I feel confused and lost at times. I confess, Lord, that I am having a hard time forgiving. I know Jesus that divorces make you unhappy, but because of the hardness of men's hearts and if adultery is committed you have permitted it. Father, I asked that any sins that I have committed, you would forgive me. I repent of my disobedience, stubborn, and rebellious ways. I ask that you wash me in the blood of the lamb.

Father, I know people say that, with time, I will heal, but you own time, you hold time, and you are time, the beginning and the end, so Father, today, I ask that you will heal me physically, spiritually, mentally, financially, and emotionally. I arrest every tormenting demon by the blood of Jesus and command them to leave me in Jesus' name. I bind every spirit of depression, anxiety, stress, loneliness, bitterness, confusion, fear, jealousy, witchcraft, vagabond, infirmity, schizophrenia, anger, and hatred. I bind every mind controlling demon, spirit of pride, passivity, rejection, every neglecting spirit, spirit of sadness, and deep hurt. I command, in the name of Jesus, and by the power of his blood, to loose me and leave me and go to the pits of hell forever.

I decree and declare that every ungodly soul tie is broken. I decree every curse spoken over my life or every curse or cursed being that I affiliated myself with is broken. I decree that every perverse spirit, Jezebel spirit, incubus and succubus spirit is broken off my life in the name of Jesus.

I decree I am healed, I am blessed, I am a royal priesthood, I am a holy nation, and God has chosen. I decree I will not be bitter, walk in self-pity or anger, I decree I will love as Jesus loves. I decree I am the joint heir to the Father's kingdom, so I want for nothing. I decree that I have life and life more abundantly. I decree I have the bloodline of Jesus. John 3:16 states, "For God so loved the world that he gave his only begotten Son, that whosoever believeth in him should not perish, but has everlasting life."

Therefore, through the agape love that has been shown by the Father. I am healed and delivered in Jesus' name, and I have everlasting life. I decree that every cell in my body that has collected a memory of tragic pain is cleansed and healed in Jesus' name; from my childhood up until now. I decree my mind will not replay painful memories over and over to torment me and I will not be reminded of tragic pain. I am healed in the name of Jesus.

I decree Ephesians 4:31-32 over my life; "Let all bitterness, and wrath, and anger, and clamour, and evil speaking, be put away from me with all malice: And be ye kind one to another tenderhearted, forgiving one another, even as God for Christ's sake hath forgiven me." I declare I forgive those that hurt me, and I declare my life is just beginning and the old has passed away in the Name of Jesus (KJV).

If you're to be a slave to someone, that someone will be Christ. Refuse to be a slave to man, but submit to be a slave to love, for God is love. Love doesn't abuse!

*Have you been abused emotionally, spiritually, physically, financially, or verbally?

*Are you struggling with leaving your abuser? If so, look deep within yourself and ask yourself why am I struggling to leave?

*Do you have a safety back up plan when things get dangerously out of hand?

National Domestic Violence: 1-800-799-7233

Reflection:_____
_____
_____
_____
_____
_____
_____
_____
_____
_____
_____
_____
_____

Lakeia M. Smith

Chapter 8 ~ Me Vs. ME

After the divorce, just as the Lord said, the ordination was next. I did not want this to happen because I knew the next step was relocation and for some reason, I tried to convince myself if I didn't get ordained, then I wouldn't have to move. Of course, this was a silly thought, but I still tried my best to convince my spiritual father I didn't need to be ordained. However, being the loving and awesome man of God, he was, my Great Late Apostle, my spiritual father insisted that I be ordained along with another sister in Christ. June 28, 2016, I was ordained at City of Life Ministries in Grovetown, Georgia by Apostle Fred Turner in the prophetic office. It was a beautiful ceremony, and we had so much support. My Apostle was so proud, and my mother was just as proud, if not more.

It felt as if time sped up after the ordination. I immediately received a phone call stating I had to move or sign a lease. At this point, I was a single mother, with no extra income and I needed to be able to financially pay $1150.00 a month for my lease and utility expenses, at the same time continue to pay my car note, car insurance, and daycare. I knew this would be really tight for me, but because I did not want to move, I was willing to work multiple jobs. I started applying for several different jobs. I applied anywhere from billing and accounting to regular customer service jobs. At the time, I only had one job, and I loved my job, but it was not enough to sustain me and my children, financially. No matter what basic job I applied for I could not get it. God would not allow me to receive any additional income. He said I had to move and that was it.

    I could see myself as Jonah at the time, being told to do something by God and trying my best not to do it. I knew fighting against what the Father had spoken to me would get me nowhere. This was a fight I already knew I could not win. Once I submitted, the Holy Spirit told me not to take any of my furniture but to only take our clothes. I packed me and my children's clothes. I gave away my furniture, from my forks and spoons up to my sofa, and beds. August 5, 2016, I resigned from my job, and on August 6, 2016, I packed my car up with my boys and jumped on I-20 towards Cartersville. Everything in me cried. I did not want to make this move, but I knew I had no choice. I had negative thoughts saying, "Nobody will want to be with you. You're a single mother with two kids, from two different marriages."

    Day and night, I beat myself up. I was again back in a place of shame, sadness, and rejection. This time it was not a man that rejected me, but I rejected myself. I would have moments alone and would cry because of feeling like I failed my children. I felt I failed them by allowing them to witness horrible behavior in the relationships I'd partaken in, and now I'm moving them away from their fathers and I could not explain to them why. I believed they were angry with me for moving, but again I knew if I stayed in Augusta at that time, it was not a safe place for any of us.

During this time of transition, I did some deep soul searching. I prayed and fasted asking the Lord why I chose to date and marry those men. I married men that abused alcohol, drugs, my children, and me. What about me drew these guys to me and me to them? One day during my morning meditation, the Spirit of the Lord revealed to me the answer to my questions. He showed me my father and revealed to me the un-forgiveness I carried towards him. I realized I'm a grown woman, who still had a little girl that had Daddy Issues. God showed me how my relationship with my father mirrored the relationships I had with my ex-husbands.

I always loved my biological father, and I always had the desire to be daddy's girl. But growing up, my dad was not around because he was an addict. My dad missed my basketball games, volleyball games, and he never made any of my track meets. He missed my middle school graduation and could not afford to help my mother with school clothes, shoes, Christmas, birthdays or any holiday or school needs. My father was a true addict, and the only time we would see him is when he was tired of running the streets. After he rested, he would cook breakfast or dinner for my brothers and me to eat with him. During my junior prom, my father was not around to see me because he was out getting high. However, when I became a senior, I refused to go to my senior prom and not see my dad. After my mother helped me get dressed for my senior prom, I begged her to take me to find my father, after all this was my last prom. My mother tried to encourage me not to go look for him, but I insisted. She took me riding through the drug community where she felt he would be. When she spotted him, he was in the woods getting high. She yelled his name, and he came out the woods towards the car, high on crack. I quickly locked my door and began to cry. I heard my father say to my mother "I can't look at her." This broke my spirit. My father was too high and ashamed to see me before my prom, and I was fearful of him because I didn't want to see him high. On that night, I heard my father's voice, but I never looked into his eyes, and I am blessed to say, I've never had to see him eye to eye while he was high.

As I continued to grow, I prayed for my father daily, and I took on the weight of believing it was my responsibility to take care of my father. I've taken my father in my home numerous times. If he would not come back home for days, I would freak out and cry, call all over the city. I would call hospitals, the jail houses, ride the streets late just to find him. I told my dad he didn't have to work, I would take care of him, and he could just stay in my home and help with household chores. During my father's stay with me, he has taken my car, came home high, drunk, and beat up, and I allowed myself to become his enabler. This is the same behavior I portrayed with my ex-husbands. I was their enabler, I took on their issues, and I married the type of man my father portrayed to me. You must realize, growing up, I was not around a lot of good men. My first heartbreak came from my godfather who cheated on my godmother with her best friend, and the same thing happen to me with my first marriage. Then I married the abusive drug addicted man that my biological father portrayed. I realized at the age of 28, I needed healing and deliverance, and I still harbored un-forgiveness, and this time it was with my dad.

I was very happy the Lord showed me these things about myself because I wanted peace, I wanted deliverance in every area of my life, and I did not want to fall into the same type of abusive relationships anymore. It was time for me to break the cycle of abuse and the mindset of being an abused enabling young woman. It was time for me to transform my thoughts and examine my heart so I can be healed. It's now me verses me.

Psalms 40:1-3 *I waited patiently for the LORD; he turned to me and heard my cry. [2] He lifted me out of the slimy pit, out of the mud and mire; he set my feet on a rock and gave me a firm place to stand. [3] He put a new song in my mouth, a hymn of praise to our God. Many will see and fear the LORD and put their trust in him (NIV).*

I realized I had to forgive my dad and understand it was not my responsibility to take care of him. My job was to pray for him and love him, and where I could help, I would still help, but I could not be his mother. It is not his fault my behavior exemplified parental authority over him. I allowed myself to take that responsibility because I felt no one else cared. I love my daddy and thought I could help him become the father that I needed. I realized I am not God, and I did not allow my Heavenly Father to be a true father in my life because of my relationship with my earthly father. I spoke with my father and expressed to him how much I loved him, and I apologized for trying to make him be the father I wanted. I apologized for refusing to understand this was his life and he was responsible for his choices not me. I apologized for enabling him and trying to control him like a child, so much I would cry and scream at him for not coming home and for getting high.

Again, this was his life. I apologized for holding him to a standard that he could not keep, because even as a young man growing up, he did not have a father in his life. I had to come to the understanding that my dad fathered us to the best of his knowledge. People can only teach you as much as they have studied, and experienced. No one can truly give to you what they have never received, or experienced, and sometimes they do not have the capacity to give you what you desire. I had to understand my father loved me but did not have the capacity to father me like I desired because he never received the full fathering he needed. Today my father is drug free and is saved. He's learning to trust God and he is very enthused about the word and always have questions to ask me about the bible. We have a great relationship.

While in the process of dealing with me, and I had to also ask myself for forgiveness. I needed to ask myself to forgive me for allowing abuse, for enabling others, for not loving myself like I'm supposed to love myself. I asked myself forgiveness for telling myself that no one will love me, for telling myself that I deserve to be hurt because of mistakes I made, for lying to myself saying I'm not good enough and I don't deserve the best. I forgive me!

As I continued to go through my process of dealing with me. I had one last major hurdle to jump. It was time for me to speak with my mother concerning the deep hurt I had with her. I knew this had to happen because I found myself getting angry when my mom would call me on my cell phone. There were so many times I did not want to talk to her but felt as if I had to force myself to speak with her. It was a challenge because over the years, although we would have good days and she was my support, we would argue like cats and dogs. She would say I respected everyone else except her. I would argue this is not true. I respected her but there was a wall that was between us and we could not get past it. I prayed one day driving home from work and told the Lord I could not take arguing with my mother any more, and if he did not help us, I would quit preaching because there is no way I will continue to stand in front of people with my heart heavy. I was tired. I'd been through so much but having issues with my mom impacted me more than anything I'd had faced because she was like my best friend. She had the power to hurt me in a way that no one else could just by arguing, and it's because I loved her so much and I didn't want to be disrespectful to her. However, some of the things she would say to me made me just want to fight. I realized, I received my spirit to fight both physically, and spiritually from my mom, because she is a true warrior.

After talking to the Lord about my mother, my mother and I eventually had a conversation. Truthfully, the conversation was like a cat fight. We screamed at each other. It started off in a heartbreaking way, but as we listened to the words coming out of each other's mouths, we realized that we both were hurting. I told my mother how a guy molested me when I was young. In her younger immature days, my mother would have card games at her house at night and many people came to play. I told her the details as to how he tried to force himself inside of me and I cried. He held me and told me to be quiet. He was someone I didn't know. He was not a family member. He'd just happen to come to the card game that night and somehow chose me to try and have sex with. He made me lay on my right side, pulled down my underwear, and penetrated me from the back. As I cried, he told me to be quiet, but tears flowed from my eyes. Finally, he let me go after hearing other children coming around looking for me. I later saw this man several times after that night and every time I saw him, I froze. Fear would grab me, and he would look me in my eyes and smile. I felt as if his soul would scream to me, *You better not tell anyone or I'm going to get you.* I never knew his name, but I never lost the image of his face, and to this day, I still know what he looks like.

My mother never knew what happened to me until this screaming match of a conversation we had when I was 29 years old. I finally released my molestation story to her, she cried and asked why I didn't tell her. She apologized to me and said she didn't know. For some apparent reason, all these years I thought she knew. I blamed her for having card games and causing this to happen to me. I blamed her for taking me away from my godmother and causing me to have a different life than I imagined. The truth is she really did not have any idea that this happened, and knowing my mother now, if she knew this happened to her little girl, she would have possibly killed the guy herself. My mom held me, and I cried in her arms like a baby. The little molested girl that I buried seemed to have risen back up in me that very moment and allowed her mother to love her, hold her and protect her. My mom apologized again and said,

"I'm sorry I wasn't the mother you needed. I did what I knew to do, and I need you to understand that my mother was not a mother to me."

I received this because I knew this to be true. My mom had it very rough as a child. Her mother was not there. She was abused as a child. She was raped, and these things led to a very hard life for her. But I am blessed that she tried her best to love me and my brothers, and she cleaned herself up and gave Jesus her heart to raise her kids.

It came to my attention, because of the molestation, I became sexually active at an early age. It was my way of dealing with the pain. I told myself a man has already touched me anyway so what does it matter. This is the mindset I had while growing up. No, I was not promiscuous, but for a while I did not mind having sex outside of marriage with whoever I was dating. My understanding of love was perverted because of my innocence being taken from me by a strange man. People deal with their pain differently. Some resort to drugs, some alcohol, and some become homosexuals and hate the opposite sex because of the pain the molester caused them.

There are many unhealthy ways people deal with their buried pain, and this is why we should not judge an individual without getting to know them and learning the root of their pain and confusion. The love I experienced from a young girl to an adult woman from a man was not the love of Jesus. I struggled with identifying what true love was because I had so much hurt. My perception of love was perverted. Love is not abuse, love is not molestation, love is not drug, alcohol, riches, and money. *But love is patient, love is kind. It does not envy, it does not boast, it is not proud. It does not dishonor others, it is not self-seeking, it is not easily angered, it keeps no record of wrongs. Love does not delight in evil but rejoices with the truth. It always protects, always trusts, always hopes, always perseveres (1 Corinthians 13:4-7 NIV).* I realized, if the love I receive from someone does not have these characteristics, then it is not true love.

After my confession and moment of healing with my mother, I felt something happen in my heart. The wall that was up, had now been broken, and forgiveness truly had taken place in me. The next day, we went to my mother's church, and a prophet prophesied to the both of us. He said there was a wall between us, and it was not a matter of disrespect but the wall that was there caused us not to see each other the way God wanted us to. My God, this was confirmation of what just happened the day before. This man knew nothing about the argument, the break down, the conversation, the love, and the forgiveness that had taken place between my mother and me. Now, I began to cry, and my mom grabbed the microphone and testified that the prophetic word was accurate and told the congregation the forgiving experience we'd had the day before. Today, my mom and I have a great relationship and I love her so much. She is my best friend. I was no longer angry, and today I do not become frustrated or agitated with my mom like I used to. I've been set free.

1 Peter 4:8 *Above all, love each other deeply, because love covers over a multitude of sins (NIV).*

As I continued examining myself, the Lord showed me how he sees me through his eyes. He gave me a queen's confession, and told me I am a GBQ, (God's Beautiful Queen/ Gorgeous Beautiful Queen). As I made my confession every day, I gained more understanding of the word when it states *Faith Comes by Hearing*. If people can speak negative words to you and you believe and receive them, or you speak negative words to yourself and believe and receive them, then you can do the same with positive words.

One day, I looked at myself in the mirror and spoke to the same young woman that I despised seeing at one point of my life. I prophesied to her and told her how beautiful she is, intelligent she is, I told her that she was created with purpose, and she would be one to speak God's word and help change many people's lives. I no longer despised looking at myself. I became stronger, and refused to walk with my head hanging down. I no longer compared myself to other women because I realized God took his time to make me, and when he looked at me, he said *It is good*. My confidence, self-esteem, healing, and deliverance came from deciding that I was tired of living bound, and I will do what it takes to be set free. Liberty was my goal, peace was my goal, and healing and deliverance was my goal. I recognized I'm no good for others if I don't help myself. I constantly made positive confessions and affirmations to myself. I prayed and fasted often, I confessed my struggles and refused to allow shame to cover me. I examined myself daily by reading the word of God. The Holy Spirit instructed me to pray Roman 12:9-21 in order to help me with my character, attitude, and to help me truly forgive. As I prayed this prayer daily, I noticed hidden anger was replaced by love, and true forgiveness radiated from me.

Prayer: *Father thank you for seeing me as royalty and allowing me to see that anything outside of royalty is a lie. Thank you for helping me to deal with me. The things my father and mother may or may have not done I forgive them for. Father help me to let love be without dissimulation to abhor that which is evil and cleave to that which is good. Teach me to be kindly affectionate to others with brotherly love. Help me to not be slothful in business and fervent in spirit serving the Lord. I will rejoice in hope, be patient in tribulation and continue instant in prayer.*

Help me to distribute to the necessity of saints and be given to hospitality. I will bless them which persecute me, and curse not. I will rejoice with them that do rejoice, and weep with them that weep. Father, I desire to be of the same mind, one toward another. Minding not high things but condescend to men of low estate. I do not want to be wise in my own conceits. I will recompense to no man evil for evil and will provide things honest in the sight of all men. If it be possible, as much that lieth within me, I will live peaceably with all men. I will not avenge myself, but rather give place unto wrath: for it is written, Vengeance is mine; I will repay, saith the Lord. Therefore, if my enemy hunger, I will feed him; if he thirsts, I will give him drink: for in so doing I shalt heap coals of fire on his head. I will not be overcome of evil, but I will overcome evil with good.

I command and bind all generational, hereditary, and spirits that has entered my life through un-forgiveness to be cast out in the name of Jesus. Father, I know when I fall you do not forget me but wait for me to come back to you. I want to forgive like you forgive, I understand I may not forget the things which have happened to me, but I still can forgive whole heartedly, and this is good for me and for the other parties. Thank you, for rebuilding broken relationships and allowing beauty to come out of my brokenness and purpose out of my pain. You are such a great artist, Father and I thank you for my new beginning. Help me to continue to strive for holiness and righteousness in Jesus' name, Amen.

Fallen doesn't mean forgotten.
Forgiveness doesn't mean forgetting.
But fallen + forgiveness + faith = peaceful future.

*Do you feel the individuals you court and/or marry are similar?

*Have you taken the time to look into yourself and ask God if there are any similar cycles in your life that needs to be broken?

Reflection:_____

Lakeia M. Smith

Queens Royal Confession

I am God's Beautiful Queen **(GBQ)**, I am a Gorgeous Beautiful Queen. Proverbs 3:15 states, I am more precious than rubies: and all the things one can desire are not to be compared unto me. God made me perfect and I love myself. 1 Peter 2:9 states, I am a chosen generation, royal priesthood, a holy nation, I am a peculiar person. I am a woman with a meek and lowly spirit. I am swift to hear, slow to speak, and slow to anger. I am strong, confident and intelligent, a woman of prayer, a woman with morals. I respect myself and others. I am an example of greatness. I will be holy because God is holy. I can do all things through Christ which strengthens me. For I am bought with a price: therefore, I must glorify God in my body, and in my spirit, which is His. I will pray for my brother, sisters, and enemies and love them with the love of Christ. God did not make a mistake when he created me., I was born with purpose, and I have been set a part for a time such as this. I am prosperous and everything my hands touch will flourish. I will walk in the power of the Holy Spirit. I will fulfill my destiny, and there is nothing that the enemy can do to stop me or harm me. I am covered by the blood of Jesus. In Jesus' name, I receive these words in and over my life.

I am a Queen!

Kings Royal Confession

I am a **King Created by The King** (KCK). I am a handsome Man. I am a mighty man of valor. God made me perfect and I love myself. 1 Peter 2:9 states, I am a chosen generation, royal priesthood, a holy nation, I am a peculiar person. I am a humble man, I am swift to hear, slow to speak, and slow to anger. I am strong and intelligent, a man of prayer, a man with morals. I will be on guard, stand firm in faith. I am courageous and strong. I respect myself and others. I am an example of greatness. I will be holy because God is holy. I can do all things through Christ which strengthens me. For I am bought with a price: therefore, I must glorify God in my body, and in my spirit, which is His. I will pray for my brothers, sisters, and enemies and love them with the love of Christ. God did not make a mistake when he created me, I was born with purpose, and Romans 8:19 states, I am one of the sons the earth is waiting to reveal. I am prosperous and everything my hands touch will flourish. I will walk in the power of the Holy Spirit. I will fulfill my destiny, and there is nothing that the enemy can do to stop me or harm me. I am covered by the blood of Jesus. In Jesus' name, I receive these words in and over my life.

I am a King!

Chapter 9 ~ Healed

A New Beginning

Today I no longer count myself out, I don't allow anyone too verbally, mentally, emotionally, physically, financially, and spiritually abuse me. I've forgiven myself, my father, mother, best friend and ex-husbands. I now have great relationships with each of these individuals. I have great conversations with my children concerning my past relationships with their fathers. I've been blessed to listen to their fathers confess the things they've done and encourage their sons not to follow their footsteps. Also, despite what the enemy tried to make me believe concerning not being truly loved by a man because of my past, the Lord sent me a Great Man of God, who prays, and fast on my behalf. A man who preaches the gospel of Jesus Christ, a man who the father has used to help cultivate the gifts in me, a man who is in tune with the precious Holy Spirit, a man who loves me unconditionally. He was someone I did not want but was who I needed, and the Lord sent him my way. Despite the fight I gave him as he pursued me due to all I was going through, he never left my side, he is my best friend and my present husband, Pastor Eugene Smith. Continue to follow us as we write about our journey courting, God, and each other.

I want to leave you with this thought. You are not your past, you are not who people say you are, you are not what they think you are, you are who God calls you. Your destiny may have been delayed but it is not denied. And what the heavenly Father has spoken over your life for you, will come to past because his word does not return to him void and he cannot lie. Remember, forgiving is the key to your healing. Despise not your dark place of pain, even though it scares you sometimes. Understand that fear pushes you to faith; faith pushes you to your place of freedom while pressure pushes you to pray and prayer pushes you to purpose. You must acknowledge your differences, your hurt, and your challenges so you can submit them to God. Once they are submitted and you surrender, Philippians 1:6, "He which hath begun a good work in you will perform it until the day of Jesus Christ." Your life is not over, and it is not too late to fulfill your purpose. You are just beginning.

Twenty Nuggets of Wisdom

1. If you're being abused, don't try to fight your battle alone. Sometimes it's hard to leave your abuser although you know it's the best decision for you and your children if you have them. If you are struggling with leaving your abuser, seek counsel and do not try to fight this battle alone. If it becomes extremely dangerous call 911 or National Domestic Violence: 1-800-799-7233.

2. Know that it's ok to cry, it's ok to say you're weak in spirit and in your flesh. Confession is the first step to healing and deliverance.

3. If you're battling with suicidal thoughts, tell someone how you feel. Challenge yourself to change your thoughts. The enemy desires you to take your life; don't give him the satisfaction. Know that God loves you, and there are people that love you and need you. ***2 Corinthians 10:5-7*** *Casting down imaginations, and every high thing that exalteth itself against the knowledge of God and bringing into captivity every thought to the obedience of Christ (KJV).* National Suicide Hotline Contact: 1-800-273-8255

4. Remember to do the first thing first. Don't worry about step 2 if you have not completed step 1. Sometimes looking too far ahead will allow you to become anxious and looking far behind will cause you to feel shame for your past. Stay in the present, for it is a gift and do the first thing first.

5. Change your circle. Sometimes your present friends are not the best support during your positive transition. They may not understand your transition and may not understand the vision God has given you for your life. Be okay with letting them go. Sometimes you have to have a season of positive selfishness. *1 Corinthians 15:33* Do not be misled: "Bad company corrupts good character (NIV)."

6. Don't be unequally yoked in any relationship. If your friends, or companions are not trying to walk the positive, successful, and holy road you desire to walk, do not connect yourself with them.

7. Before taking a covenant in marriage, evaluate your companion's life, his/her family life, and his /her

relationships with his/her family and friends, his/her values, morals and finances. If they do not line up with the word of God or with the positive vision you have for your life, do not take covenant, because once you take covenant, all of your companion's challenges, family curses or blessings will become yours.

8. Be willing to examine yourself to recognize negative cycles/patterns in your life. This will help you know what to target in prayer and allow you to take the necessary steps to break them. Negative patterns and cycles can be broken, and new ones can be created.

9. Write your goals and place them where you can see them daily. Know that every positive step of change you make is important, do not despise your small beginning. Take one step at a time, one day at a time, and before you know it you will reach your goals.

10. If you are struggling with forgiving those that hurt you. Write your pain down and tell them why. It doesn't matter if they are alive, have passed away, live near or far. Get your feelings out on paper or confide in someone and let them know why you're

having a hard time forgiving. Once you've done this step, confess out of your mouth that you forgive that person and say the name. Continue to push yourself to do this daily until you truly have forgiveness in your heart. Forgiving those that hurt you frees you.

11. Look yourself in the mirror and say positive confessions and affirmations. It's important you minister to yourself. Be willing to date yourself. Make time daily for you.

12. Pray and read your word daily.

13. Don't compare yourself to other people. Remember you are precious, God took his time to form you in his image, and he made you different on purpose because he placed a gift in you that he knew the world needs. Now the world is waiting on you to release it. If God wanted everyone to be the same, he would create us with the same personality and characteristics.

14. You are a treasure that has been hidden, but your time has come where your light can no longer be hid.

15. When you are feeling lonely, depressed, or feel you're suffering heavily, do not isolate yourself. Push yourself to church, push yourself to be amongst those that can pray for you and encourage you. You can draw strength from others.

16. Don't be ashamed of your testimony. Someone needs to hear that you struggled but made it through. Your testimony is a verbal expression of your war scars, you overcame many battles you thought you would lose.

17. If you do not like how things are going in your life, only you have the power to change the course you're traveling. Don't be your own enemy, don't be your own bully.

18. Don't allow the pain and the fear of your past to prophesy to your future. The Holy Spirit is the spirit of truth. Anything opposite of what the spirit of truth speaks is a lie. Refuse to be trapped by the lie and allow yourself to rest in the truth.

19. Allow the Holy Spirit to be your best friend. Become as a child again and talk to him. Although you can't see him, you can hear him, and you can feel him. He will reveal the kingdom secrets to you, and the enemy's plans to you. This is why you can never lose a war. You have a mole in the enemy's camp, the Holy Ghost!

20. You Are Victorious! You Are Favored and You Have Favor! **Faith-Activated-Over-R**eciprocity!

Bible Scriptures

Isaiah 41:10-13 *Fear thou not; for I am with thee: be not dismayed; for I am thy God: I will strengthen thee; yea I will help thee; yea I will uphold thee with the right hand of my righteousness (KJV).*

Hebrews 12:29 *Our God is a consuming fire (KJV).*

John 3:5-7 *Jesus answered, I assure you, most solemnly I tell you, unless a man is born of water and [even] the Spirit, he cannot [ever] enter the kingdom of God. What is born of [from] the flesh is flesh [of the physical is physical]; and what is born of the Spirit is spirit. Marvel not [do not be surprised, astonished] at My telling you, You must all be born anew (from above) (AMP).*

Psalms 51:17 *My sacrifice [the sacrifice acceptable] to God is a broken spirit; a broken and a contrite heart [broken down with sorrow for sin and humbly and thoroughly penitent], such, O God, You will not despise (AMP).*

Isaiah 57:15 *For thus says the high and lofty One -- "He Who inhabits eternity, Whose name is Holy: I dwell in the high and holy place, but with him also who is of a thoroughly penitent and humble spirit, to revive the spirit of the humble and to revive the heart of the thoroughly penitent [bruised with sorrow for sin](AMP).*

2 Corinthians 11:14 *And no marvel, for Satan himself is transformed into an angel of light (KJV).*

1 Corinthians 14:33 *For God is not the author of confusion, but of peace, as in all churches of the saints (KJV).*

1 John 1:9 *If we confess our sins, he is faithful and just and will forgive us our sins and purify us from all unrighteousness (NIV).*

Proverbs 23:7 *For as he thinketh in his heart, so is he.*

Jeremiah 3:14 *Turn, O backsliding children, saith the LORD; for I am married unto you: and I will take you one of a city, and two of a family, and I will bring you to Zion (KJV).*

Proverbs 24:16 *For a just man falleth seven times, and riseth up again: but the wicked shall fall into mischief (KJV).*

1 Corinthians 11:24-26 *states* [24] *and when he had given thanks, he broke it and said, "This is my body, which is for you; do this in remembrance of me."* [25] *In the same way, after supper he took the cup, saying, "This cup is the new covenant in my blood; do this, whenever you drink it, in remembrance of me."* [26] *For whenever you eat this bread and drink this cup, you proclaim the Lord's death until he comes (KJV).*

Psalm 38:9 *All my longings lie open before you, Lord; my sighing is not hidden from you (NIV).*

1 Peter 5:7 *Casting all your care upon him; for he careth for you (KJV).*

Proverbs 11:14 *Where no counsel is, the people fall: but in the multitude of counselors there is safety (KJV).*

Hebrews 10:25 *Not forsaking the assembling of ourselves together, as the manner of some is; but exhorting one another: and so much the more, as ye see the day approaching (KJV).*

Psalms 69 *¹ Save me, O God, for the waters have come up to my neck. ² I sink in the miry depths, where there is no foothold. I have come into the deep waters; the floods engulf me. ³ I am worn out calling for help; my throat is parched. My eyes fail, looking for my God. ⁴ Those who hate me without reason outnumber the hairs of my head; many are my enemies without cause, those who seek to destroy me. I am forced to restore what I did not steal. ⁵ You, God, know my folly; my guilt is not hidden from you (NIV).*

Matthew 6:26 *Look at the birds of the air; they do not sow or reap or store away in barns, and yet your heavenly Father feeds them (KJV).*

Philippians 4:19 *But my God shall supply all your need according to his riches in glory by Christ Jesus (KJV).*

Psalm 37:4-5 *Delight thyself also in the LORD: and he shall give thee the desires of thine heart. ⁵ Commit thy way unto the LORD; trust also in him; and he shall bring it to pass (KJV).*

Matthew 4:4 *But he answered and said, It is written, Man shall not live by bread alone, but by every word that proceedeth out of the mouth of God (KJV).*

Zechariah 3:3-4 *Now Joshua was dressed in filthy clothes as he stood before the angel. ⁴ The angel said to those who were* *standing before him, "Take off his filthy clothes". Then he said to Joshua, "See, I have taken away your sin, and I will put fine garments on you (KJV)."*

Matthew 6:33 *states "Seek ye first the kingdom of God and his righteousness and all these things shall be added unto me". I make the decision to seek the Kings righteousness and his kingdom (KJV).*

Isaiah 54:17 *No weapon that is formed against thee shall prosper (KJV).*

John 10:10 *"The thief cometh not, but for to steal, and to kill, and to destroy (KJV)."*

2 Timothy 3 *But evil men and seducers shall wax worse and worse, deceiving, and being deceive. But continue thou in the things which thou hast learned and hast been assured of, knowing of whom thou hast learned them; And that from a child thou hast known the holy scriptures, which are able to make thee wise unto salvation through faith which is in Christ Jesus (KJV).*

Mark 9:24 *"Lord I believe, but help my unbelief (KJV)."*

Hebrews 4:16 *"Let us therefore come boldly unto the throne of grace, that we may obtain mercy, and find grace to help in time of need (KJV),"*

2 Peter 1:3 *His divine power has given us everything we need for a godly life through our knowledge of him who called us by his own glory and goodness (NIV).*

1 Corinthians 7:15-17 *But if the unbeliever leaves, let it be so. The brother or the sister is not bound in such circumstances; God has called us to live in peace. ¹⁶ How do you know, wife, whether you will save your husband? Or, how do you know, husband, whether you will save your wife (NIV)?*

Psalms 46:10 *Be still and know that I am God (KJV).*

James 5:16 *"Confess your faults one to another, and pray one for another, that ye may be healed (KJV).*

Ephesians 4:31-32 *over my life; "Let all bitterness, and wrath, and anger, and clamour, and evil speaking, be put away from me with all malice: And be ye kind one to another tenderhearted, forgiving one another, even as God for Christ's sake hath forgiven me (KJV).*

Psalms 40:1-3 *I waited patiently for the* LORD*; he turned to me and heard my cry. ² He lifted me out of the slimy pit, out of the mud and mire; he set my feet on a rock and gave me a firm place to stand. ³ He put a new song in my mouth, a hymn of praise to our God. Many will see and fear the* LORD *and put their trust in him (NIV).*

1 Peter 4:8 *Above all, love each other deeply, because love covers over a multitude of sins (NIV).*

1 Corinthians 13:4-7 *Love is patient, love is kind. It does not envy, it does not boast, it is not proud. It does not dishonor others, it is not self-seeking, it is not easily angered, it keeps no record of wrongs. Love does not delight in evil but rejoices with the truth. It always protects, always trusts, always hopes, always perseveres (NIV).*

Roman 12:9-21 [9] *Let love be without dissimulation. Abhor that which is evil; cleave to that which is good.* [10] *Be kindly affectioned one to another with brotherly love; in honour preferring one another;* [11] *Not slothful in business; fervent in spirit; serving the Lord;* [12] *Rejoicing in hope; patient in tribulation; continuing instant in prayer;* [13] *Distributing to the necessity of saints; given to hospitality.* [14] *Bless them which persecute you: bless, and curse not.* [15] *Rejoice with them that do rejoice, and weep with them that weep.* [16] *Be of the same mind one toward another. Mind not high things but condescend to men of low estate. Be not wise in your own conceits.* [17] *Recompense to no man evil for evil. Provide things honest in the sight of all men.* [18] *If it be possible, as much as lieth in you, live peaceably with all men.* [19] *Dearly beloved, avenge not yourselves, but rather give place unto wrath: for it is written, Vengeance is mine; I will repay, saith the Lord.* [20] *Therefore if thine enemy hunger, feed him; if he thirst, give him drink: for in so doing thou shalt heap coals of fire on his head.* [21] *Be not overcome of evil, but overcome evil with good* (KJV).

1 Peter 4:8 *Above all, love each other deeply, because love covers over a multitude of sins (NIV).*

1 Corinthians 15:33 *Do not be misled: "Bad company corrupts good character (NIV)."*

2 Corinthians 10:5-7 *Casting down imaginations, and every high thing that exalteth itself against the knowledge of God, and bringing into captivity every thought to the obedience of Christ (NIV).*

About the Author

Lakeia M. Smith is a compassionate person and loves God with all her heart. She has been through many attacks from the devil which only strengthened her and motivated her to get closer to God. She is a minister of the Gospel of Jesus Christ, and the visionary of God's Beautiful Queens (GBQs)/Gorgeous Beautiful Queens, which aids young women to see the beauty within them and to see themselves as the holy and pure Queens God created them to be.

Ms. Smith is a powerful woman of faith endowed with the anointing in the prophetic as an intercessor, seer, and discerner of the voice of God. As a child, Lakeia always had interesting behaviors. Her behaviors were not of a normal child that acted out in a negative way, but behaviors that expressed there were special gifts within her.

She has dedicated her life to live as a true example through the Word of God, making great sacrifices for the benefit and spiritual wellbeing of others. Lakeia desires to see God's people healed and delivered from brokenness. She believes if God did it for her he will do it for you.

From Bondage To Liberty, Abused But Still Anointed is her first published book.